P9-DNN-118

"Whether she's giving me tips and advice on how to cook a good fish dish, the secrets to a good kitchen, or her favorite indulgence of brioche on a Sunday morning, it's clear to see that a love of good food is ingrained in her."—Women's Way

homemade

In *Homemade*, Clodagh McKenna, acclaimed cook, writer and television presenter, has created an invaluable kitchen companion. Whether you are searching for the perfect recipe for a special occasion, need inspiration for a dinner-party menu, or simply want guidance on how to make delicious strawberry jam, this book is packed with easy-to-follow, mouth-watering recipes, friendly advice, and helpful household tips.

There are fantastic ideas for using pantry ingredients to create interesting everyday meals and enticing lunchboxes, as well as wonderful recipes for lazy brunches, relaxed celebrations with family and friends, decadent afternoon teas, and cozy fireside suppers. For more formal occasions, Clodagh has devised simple, yet irresistible, dinner-party menus for every season, accompanied by suggestions for stunning table settings and homemade edible gifts for guests.

Whatever you are planning to serve, *Homemade* will prove a wonderful guide to good food and easy entertaining as well as a reassuring, fail-safe hand in the kitchen.

homemade

homemade

Irresistible Homemade Recipes
for Every Occasion

Clodagh McKenna

Photography by Alberto Peroli

Kyle Books

To Erin McKenna
My business partner, best buddy,
and lucky for me married my
brother. You make everything possible...
I can never thank you enough xx

Published in 2011 by Kyle Books
an imprint of Kyle Cathie Limited
www.kylebooks.com

Distributed by National Book Network
4501 Forbes Blvd., Suite 200
Lanham, MD 20706
Phone: (800) 462-6420
Fax: (301) 429-5746
custserv@nbnbooks.com

First published in Great Britain in 2010 by Kyle Cathie Limited

ISBN 978-1-906868-46-8

© 2010 by Clodagh McKenna
Design © 2010 by Kyle Cathie Limited
Photography © 2010 by Alberto Peroli

All rights reserved. No reproduction, copy or transmission of this
publication may be made without written permission. No paragraph
of this publication may be reproduced, copied or transmitted save
with written permission or in accordance with the provisions of
the Copyright Act 1956 (as amended). Any person who does any
unauthorised act in relation to this publication may be liable to
criminal prosecution and civil claims for damages.

Project Managed by Blue Dragonfly, www.bluedragonfly-uk.com
(Caroline West, Editorial; Mark Latter, Design)
Photography by Alberto Peroli
Food styling by Clodagh McKenna
Home economy and props styling by Polly Webb-Wilson
Production by Gemma John

Clodagh McKenna is hereby identified as the author of this work in
accordance with Section 77 of the Copyright, Designs and Patents
Act 1988.

Library of Congress Control Number: 2011920341

Printed in China by 1010 Printing International Ltd.

Note to Reader
—All spoon measurements are level unless otherwise stated.
—Eggs are medium unless otherwise stated.

contents

introduction

My starting point for this book was the *Housekeeper's Guide* that my mum was given when she first set up home. She still has it—a huge, heavy book with a burlap cover. It's battered round the edges from constant use, and favorite recipe pages are covered in sticky fingerprints. As a child, I used it for pressing flowers, and occasionally insects, but for my mum it was like a housekeeping bible, stuffed with recipes, handy tips, and sound advice.

This book is not just for new brides, but also for single dads, independent women, couples, and everyone in between. There are ideas on entertaining, cooking for yourself, friends, and family; and organizing and decorating your home. The book is packed with handy household tips and advice on everything from table settings to how to select the perfect cheese board.

The chapters reflect my own approach to cooking and home-making. I prefer to use foods and flowers that are in season. I am a great believer in maintaining old traditions, such as preserving fruits and vegetables in the fall to use through the winter. I love the informality of a lazy brunch as much as the elegant formality of afternoon tea; I love the sophistication of apéritifs just as much as curling up for a cozy fireside supper. Our lives are very varied: I wanted to reflect this in the chapters, finding food and ideas to suit every mood and occasion.

My aim is for this book to become a kitchen companion to you in the same way that my mum's housekeeping manual was to her. A faithful friend you can turn to when you need good solid advice on stocking up the pantry and on storage, inspiration for dinner-party menus, ideas for something nutritious for a lunchbox, a recipe for jam, or maybe even just somewhere you can press fresh flowers!

Clodagh McKenna

I love using seasonal produce like fresh summer raspberries.

Manage the storage space in your kitchen so that the cabinets are never bare or packed with items that are out of date.

I think it's amazing how a certain taste can become special and captivate your heart.

simple everyday

the well-fed pantry

preserved

the envied lunchbox

a guide to cheese

the well-fed pantry

Hands up anyone who has an out-of-date product in their kitchen cabinets. Keep your hands up if it's over six months out of date...and twelve months?

We all do it: stuff the cabinets full, forget what's at the back, and then buy stuff we've already got. However, a little organization makes a world of difference. I divide my cabinets into four different areas: oils and vinegars; dried foods (including pasta, flour, rice, legumes, sugar, and salt); canned foods (tomatoes, vegetables, fruit, and fish); and jams and preserves. If you're like me, you will have core ingredients that you use all the time; this is your starting point.

Do a monthly cabinet check, or, if you want to be really organized, keep a list on the inside of your cabinet door of what's low and what you need.

We don't all have the luxury of a walk-in pantry, but in this chapter I'll show you how to manage the space you have so that your kitchen cabinets will never be bare or packed with stuff that is out of date. You need to be honest about what you do cook, though. There's no point buying exotic ingredients if you don't get round to making the dishes. Start a minimal list and add to it as you go along. Do a monthly cabinet check, or, if you want to be really organized, keep a list on the inside of your cabinet door of what's low and what you need.

Cabinet love is good. Have a thorough clean-out. Here are three incentives for doing so: one, it saves you money; two, it means there is always something in the cabinet if you want to whip up a meal in no time; and three, you know that what's in there isn't going to make you unwell.

simple everyday

one

two

three

on the shelf

shelf one:

flours, sugars,
rising agents, etc.

shelf two:

spices, nuts, dried fruits,
oils, vinegars, canned
goods, etc.

shelf three:

pasta, rice, legumes,
noodles, etc.

preserved

I once made a batch of apple jelly and took a jar home to my Dad. As he took off the lid, he became quite emotional. The smell and taste of the jelly, which was exactly like his mum's, had brought a flood of childhood memories rushing back.

I think it's incredible how a taste can get to your heart as well as your taste buds. Last winter I opened a jar of preserved lemons to add to a chicken tagine. As soon as I cut into the fruit, the aroma transported me straight back to the market place in Italy where I'd bought the lemons the summer before. There's something magical about squirreling away the season's surplus fruit and vegetables along with our memories in a glass jar. Preserving is an instinct: it helps us feel a little bit self-sufficient, as though we can provide for our friends and family. Every culture in the world has found ways to do it—lemons in North Africa, vegetables in Italy, walnuts in Iran, jams and chutneys in Ireland. The recipes in this section are from as far afield as North Africa, South America, and Italy.

For very little effort, preserves provide a large reward. Maybe that's why they make such good gifts. They look great, they make us feel good, they taste delicious, and they evoke powerful memories—that's a lot to store in a glass jar.

tips on preserving

- Only fill each jar to within ¼in of the top.

- If you wish to reduce the amount of sugar you use when making jam, substitute half of the quantity with honey.

- For non-liquid foods, it's important to remove any trapped air bubbles from the top of the jar. To do this, skim the top of the preserve with a knife.

- Wash preserving jars well and then sterilize them by placing in a hot oven for about an hour.

italian preserved carrots

cook's tip

tasty alternatives

Have a go at substituting these vegetables for the carrots: fennel bulb, zucchini, artichokes, or green beans.

This recipe was given to me by Michelle Fuerst, who is known as the "Pickling Queen" in California. The carrots are perfectly crisp and the spices provide great flavor. In Italy, they eat preserved vegetables as part of their apéritif.

serves 4

3 large carrots
1 onion

For the brine
1 cup cider vinegar
¼ cup champagne vinegar
3 cups water
1 teaspoon sea salt
1 teaspoon sugar
1 teaspoon fennel seeds
1 teaspoon coriander seeds
1 whole dried chile pepper
12 bay leaves

Peel the carrots and cut them diagonally into pieces, about ⅛in thick.

Cut the onion in half and slice into half moons, about ½in thick. Set the carrots and onion to one side.

Put all the brine ingredients in a saucepan and bring to a boil over medium heat, stirring occasionally.

Once at a slow boil, stir in the sliced onion and cook for a further 5 minutes. Remove the onion with a slotted spoon, and let cool.

When the brine is again at a boil, add the carrots and cook for about 5 minutes. Remove the carrots with the slotted spoon and spread them out to cool.

Once the brine and vegetables have cooled, put them in a storage container and refrigerate. The preserved carrots should last for a few weeks in the fridge.

homemade ketchup

Homemade ketchup is so super-simple to make and the taste is far more delicious than the store-bought version. It's one of the recipes at the children's camp at my cooking school and they love it! Make a big batch every couple of months because it will last in the refrigerator for that length of time.

makes 6 cups

¾ cup + 2 tablespoons cider vinegar
1 bay leaf
½ teaspoon ground coriander
½ teaspoon ground cinnamon
7 tablespoons demerara sugar
3lb 5oz ripe tomatoes, quartered
  and seeded
1 teaspoon sea salt
1 tablespoon English mustard powder
1 garlic clove, crushed
2 teaspoons Worcestershire sauce
2 tablespoons tomato paste
½ teaspoon cornstarch (if necessary)

Put the vinegar, bay leaf, coriander, cinnamon, and sugar in a heavy-bottomed saucepan and bring to a gentle simmer.

Stir in the tomatoes, salt, mustard powder, garlic, Worcestershire sauce, and tomato paste, and bring to a boil, stirring every few minutes.

Reduce the heat and simmer for 30 minutes, adding some cornstarch to thicken, if necessary.

Remove from the heat and let cool for a few minutes. Transfer to a food processor or blender and blend until smooth. Press the sauce through a sieve into a bowl and let cool completely before bottling.

preserved

sun-dried tomatoes

If you have a glut of tomatoes at the end of the summer, then drying them is a great way of preserving the taste for the winter. They take a while to dry, but the amount of preparation required is very small.

makes 60

30 tomatoes
2 tablespoons finely chopped
    fresh rosemary
2 tablespoons finely chopped
    fresh thyme
pinch of sea salt

to prepare your tomatoes for drying
Carefully wash and dry the tomatoes.

Cut the tomatoes in half lengthwise, removing the seeds if you wish. If you remove the seeds, make sure you do not remove the pulp.

to sun-dry
Place the tomatoes skin-side down on a wire cooling rack.

Sprinkle over the salt and fresh rosemary and thyme.

Place the rack of tomatoes in a hot sheltered spot, such as a sunroom or on a sunny windowsill. Cover with a mesh food cover to keep the flies off.

It will take at least a few days of sunshine—sometimes up to 12 days—for the tomatoes to dry properly.

to oven-dry
Preheat the oven to its lowest setting.

Prepare the tomatoes as above and put the rack of tomatoes in the oven.

Bake for 6–12 hours until the tomatoes are shrivelled and dry.

to store
The best way to store sun-dried tomatoes is in glass jars. Pack the tomatoes tightly in the jars and seal with a tight-fitting lid. Place the jars in a cool dark place in the kitchen or pantry and the tomatoes will last for about 1 year.

to rehydrate
Place the tomatoes in a large bowl of water for 2 hours.

cook's tip

making sun-dried tomato pesto

Put 3¾ cups of semi sun-dried tomatoes, ⅔ cup of freshly grated Parmesan cheese, ⅔ cup of olive oil, 1 garlic clove and ½ cup of pine nuts into a blender and grind for 3 minutes or until smooth. Add more olive oil if the pesto is too thick. Pour into a sterilized jar with a tight-fitting lid and store in the refrigerator. The pesto will last for up to a month.

I serve Christmas Chutney in my café, "The Canal Café," with organic chicken-liver pâté (see page 112 for my recipe for Farmers' Market Pâté). The spiced apples cut right through the creaminess of the pâté, which is spread over toasted sourdough bread. Delicious! It's also fabulous served with a cheese board or for marinating a piece of pork.

makes 12 x scant 1 cup jars

christmas chutney

pat of butter
2 onions, sliced
2¼lb apples (a variety suitable
   for cooking, peeled, cored, and diced
2¼ cups brown sugar
10 whole cloves
1 tablespoon chile powder
⅜in piece of fresh ginger,
   peeled and grated
1¾ cups cider vinegar
1 teaspoon sea salt
1 teaspoon freshly ground
   black pepper
1 tablespoon turmeric powder

-------- cook's tip --------

harvest, preserve, give!

Make this chutney at the end of October when apples are plentiful and at their best. It will last for 6 months and gets better with age—as with all of us! Put in pretty Mason jars and give to friends and family for Christmas.

Melt the butter in a heavy-bottomed saucepan and add the onions and apples. Stir well, cover, and let cook for 5 minutes.

Stir in the sugar, cloves, chile powder, fresh ginger, cider vinegar, salt and pepper, and turmeric powder. Mix well. Cover the saucepan and let simmer over medium heat for 20 minutes.

Remove the lid, turn down the heat to low, and let cook for a further 30 minutes or until the apple has broken down and the chutney has turned a rich golden brown color. Remove from the heat and let cool before putting in sterilized jars.

summer fruit jam

I love preserving the taste of summer as we head into the chillier seasons. This gorgeous jam recipe takes about an hour to make, but will give you months of tasty pleasure... and you can vary the recipe by using different summer fruits, such as blackberries, instead.

makes approx.
6 x 1 cup jars

2¼lb raspberries, strawberries,
(cut into quarters) and loganberries
2¼lb jam or granulated sugar with added pectin
(see cook's tips opposite)
grated zest of 1 lemon

Put all the berries in a heavy-bottomed saucepan over low heat and let simmer for about 15 minutes.

Add the jam sugar and keep stirring until it dissolves completely.

Add the lemon zest. Turn up the heat and bring to a boil. Let boil until the jam begins to set.

To test if it is set, place a teaspoon of jam on a cold saucer and let cool. If it wrinkles and feels firm, the jam is adequately set.

Pour the hot jam into sterilized jars and let cool.

Cover each jar with a disc of parchment paper and a lid.

Store in a cool dry place for up to 3 months.

fig jam

In a word, fig jam for me is yummylicious...
It looks fabulous and tastes even better. It is
so good eaten with goat cheese, cured meats,
and blue cheese.

makes approx. 1 cup container

1 cup water
¾ cup sugar
12 figs, stemmed and quartered
grated zest of 1 lemon
juice of ½ lemon
1 cinnamon stick

Pour the water and sugar into a saucepan and
place over a medium heat, stirring until the sugar
has dissolved.

Add the figs to the sugar mixture along with the
lemon zest and juice and the cinnamon stick.
Stir and bring to a light simmer, leaving the lid off
the saucepan. Cook for about 1 hour or until the
mixture has thickened.

Remove from the heat, take out the cinnamon
stick, and let cool.

Store in an airtight container in the refrigerator for
about 3 months.

cook's tips

buying figs

When shopping for figs,
make sure that they are
ripe—the color of the skin
should be a deep purple
and the fruit should yield
slightly to pressure. The
best place to store figs is in
the refrigerator, as they
have an extremely short
shelf-life. Then, about an
hour before you are
planning to cook them, take
them out of the refrigerator
to bring the fruit to room
temperature.

making and using jam

• The amount of pectin to
add varies according to the
fruit used but a general
guide is about 5fl oz of
pectin stock to 4lb of fruit.

• When using pectin, follow
the package instructions.
Generally 2–4fl oz of liquid
or 2 teaspoons of dried to
each 1lb of fruit.

• If using lemon juice
rather than pectin,
2 tablespoons to 4lb of fruit
is normally adequate.

lemon curd

I was always a huge fan of lemon curd when I was a child, but it is only recently that I have started enjoying this lemon delight again and I smother everything in it!

makes 1 x 1 cup jar

5 eggs
generous ¾ cup granulated sugar
⅛ cup + 2 tablespoons lemon juice
½ stick butter, cut into small pieces
1 tablespoon grated lemon zest

Suspend a heatproof glass bowl over a saucepan of simmering water. Crack in the eggs and add the sugar and lemon juice. Whisk together until blended. Stir constantly for about 10 minutes so that the curd doesn't scramble.

Remove from the heat and push the curd into a bowl through a fine sieve to remove any lumps.

Whisk the butter into the mixture until it has melted and the mixture is smooth.

Add the lemon zest and let cool. The lemon curd will thicken as it cools.

Once the curd has cooled, cover immediately and refrigerate for up to a week.

cook's tips

wicked ways with lemon curd

• Spread on toasted brioche bread has to be one of the most heavenly ways of eating lemon curd.

• Make a delicious Victoria sponge cake by sandwiching 2 light sponges with lemon curd and whipped cream (see my recipe for Old-Fashioned Victoria Sponge on page 129 and use some lemon curd rather than jam).

• Folded through crushed meringues with some whipped cream (see my recipe for Little Lemon Meringue Angels on page 179).

• Drizzled over ice cream, shortbread cookies, or scones—is there anything that doesn't taste better with lemon curd?

preserved lemons

I love the sweetness of preserved lemons. When I lived in Italy, there was a market on my piazza and during the summer all the lemons would come up from Amalfi to be sold in boxes. I used to buy a couple of boxes every summer and preserve the lemons for the winter months. They add so much flavor to dishes...

makes 20 preserved lemon wedges

10 unwaxed lemons
9 teaspoons sea salt
10 peppercorns
10 coriander seeds
4 bay leaves
5 cloves
1 cinnamon stick

Cut 5 of the lemons into quarters and remove the seeds.

Sprinkle 1 teaspoon of salt into a sterilized jar and then press a layer of the lemon quarters on top. Cover with 2 teaspoons of salt, a couple of peppercorns and coriander seeds, a bay leaf, and a clove. Repeat this process until you reach the top of the jar.

Break the cinnamon stick in half and push both halves down the side of the jar.

Juice the remaining 5 lemons and pour the juice into the jar. Seal and put in a cool, dark place for 3 weeks before using.

The preserved lemons will last for about 3 months.

cook's tips

using preserved lemons in your cooking

• Dice a preserved lemon and add to a ½ cup of Greek yogurt and 1 tablespoon of finely chopped fresh mint. Serve with broiled lamb or chicken.

• Dice a preserved lemon and fold through couscous with some feta, black olives, fresh cilantro, and ground cinnamon and cumin, and lots of olive oil.

• Dice a couple of preserved lemons and mix well with some softened butter, crushed garlic, and fresh basil. Then, spread under the skin of a whole chicken and roast as normal.

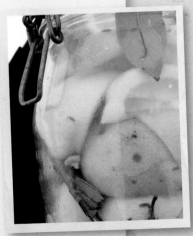

homemade limoncello

Chilled homemade limoncello in the summer—followed by a strong espresso and a chocolate truffle—is one of life's great pleasures. I usually make about 5 bottles at a time because the limoncello will last for 6 months in a bottle.

makes 4 cups

⅔ cup water
scant 1 cup superfine
  sugar
grated zest and juice of
  8 unwaxed lemons
2¾ cups vodka

Place a saucepan over a medium heat, add the water and sugar, and stir until the sugar dissolves. Bring to a boil. Reduce the heat and let simmer for 3–4 minutes until the liquid is syrupy.

Remove the pan from the heat, add the lemon zest and juice, and let cool.

Pour the vodka into the lemon syrup.

Line up the sterilized bottles and pour in the liquid. Leave in a cool, dark place for a month, shaking every day for the first week. After a month, the lemon liqueur will be ready to drink. Transfer into clean sterilized bottles.

Before serving, place the limoncello in a freezer for a couple of hours. The limoncello is best served in frozen shot glasses.

simple everyday

raspberry cordial

WI love drinking this cordial with sparkling water or adding a few drops to prosecco or cava. You can vary the recipe by replacing the raspberries with blackberries, blueberries, or strawberries.

makes 4 cups

2 cups raspberries
1¾ cups sugar
juice of ½ lemon
2 cups water

Put the raspberries, sugar, lemon, and half the water into a saucepan, and place over medium heat. Stir and cook for 5 minutes until the raspberries begin to break down.

Stir in the other half of the water, bring to a boil, and then turn down the heat and let cook for a further 15 minutes.

Transfer the raspberry mixture to a food processor and puree until you get a smooth consistency.

Strain into a bowl through a fine sieve using the back of a spoon to push the fruit through the sieve.

Pour into sterilized bottles, seal tightly, and store in the refrigerator for up to 3 weeks.

To serve, dilute 1 part raspberry cordial with 4 parts sparkling water.

the envied lunchbox

Let me ask you a question: why bother with a lunchbox? Maybe because it tastes better than a take-out sandwich? Or you know it's healthier or it brightens your morning knowing you've got a fabulous lunch to look forward to?

I ask the question because, let's face it, preparing a lunchbox does take a bit of effort, but I really believe it's worth it. You spend all morning dealing with the phone, with emails, with other people. Lunch is your time—this is something you do for yourself, so it needs to be great. Let's take a look at the lunchbox itself. You need sections in the box to keep things separate, as well as a little container with a good seal for your pickle relishes and dips. Pack a cloth napkin—it saves on paper—and a small knife for cold, cooked meats and fruit. If you're one of those people who falls asleep at the computer after a carby lunch (guilty!), try experimenting with salads or a hearty vegetable soup. If you do a roast on Sunday, put aside some meat and make a delicious couscous for your lunchbox.

I really looked forward to lunch when I worked at farmers' markets because the stall-holders would all swap food. Why not try this at work? Find a lunchbox buddy or even start a lunchbox round robin, where one person brings something new in each day. It's great trying new things and makes lunch a really sociable occasion. And, remember, lunch has to be gorgeous as well as good for you, so always pack a treat, like some Chocolate and Hazelnut Drops in this chapter.

tips for packing your children's lunchboxes

make those sandwiches fun

If you decide to pack a traditional sandwich, try cutting the bread into fun shapes using a cookie cutter. You'll be amazed at how a boring cheese sandwich will get gobbled up when shaped into a flower or dinosaur!

make eating fruit fun!

Make colorful skewers with bite-size pieces of fruit. Kids love smoothies and they are packed with vitamins. Try my Peach and Honey Smoothie on page 44.

dip it!

Kids love dipping stuff. For an easy and nutritious lunch snack, cut vegetables into sticks and serve with a delicious homemade hummus. Try my Pink Hummus on page 176.

vegetable chips

Vegetable chips are a healthy and tasty snack—a really lovely treat to look forward to during the day when you are plodding along at work. They are also a great alternative in children's lunchboxes.

makes 4 small bags of chips

2 parsnips
2 beets
2 sweet potatoes
2 tablespoons olive oil
sea salt and freshly ground black pepper

Preheat the oven to 375°F.

Peel all the vegetables, using a vegetable peeler or mandolin, and slice them diagonally into wafer-thin chips. Spread out on a dish towel or some paper towels to remove excess moisture.

Place all the vegetables in a bowl. Season with salt and pepper, and pour over the olive oil. Toss with your hands to coat evenly.

Arrange the vegetables in a single layer on a baking sheet. Roast in the oven on the lowest rack for 20 minutes, turning them over halfway through. Keep an eye on them, as they may not need the full time— they are ready when the parsnips and sweet potatoes are golden brown.

Spread out on paper towels until cool and crisp.

the envied lunchbox

spiced butternut squash soup

I love butternut squash soup, especially cooked with these spices. It's also fabulous with smoked bacon or nutmeg. Recently, I was treated to butternut squash soup with roasted porcini mushrooms and crushed hazelnuts—divine.

serves 6

¼ stick butter
½ small squash (just over 1lb), seeded and chopped into ¾in pieces
⅔ cup chopped onion
1 garlic clove, crushed
1 tablespoon ground cumin
2 cups hot chicken stock
generous ⅓ cup half and half cream
sea salt and freshly ground black pepper
small bunch of fresh cilantro, finely chopped

Melt the butter in a heavy-bottomed saucepan and add the squash, onion, and garlic. Cover and let simmer for about 15 minutes, stirring occasionally.

Add the ground cumin and sauté for a further 5 minutes.

Stir in the chicken stock and bring the soup to a boil. When the squash is tender (about 10 minutes), stir in the cream and let simmer for a minute.

Ladle the soup into a blender and puree until it reaches a smooth consistency. Season to taste.

Serve hot, stirring in the fresh cilantro just before serving.

········ cook's tip ········

making stock for soup

• For beef stock, brown marrow bones either by roasting or frying them. When they are browned, add chopped onion, celery, and carrots with a whole bulb of garlic, and cover with water. Add a spoonful of tomato paste, a splash of red wine, thyme, a bay leaf, and black pepper. Simmer gently for 2 hours.

• For chicken stock, replace the marrow bones with a chicken carcass, the red wine with white wine, and the thyme with a bouquet garni.

• For fish stock, add fish bones to vegetables like leek and fennel and flavor with dill or a bouquet garni.

orzo vegetable soup

I started making this delicious soup when I lived in Turin in northern Italy. The winters were fiercely cold there. I craved warm, healthy, comforting dishes, and this one became my weekly lunch companion.

serves 6

2 tablespoons olive oil
1 onion, finely chopped
2 garlic cloves, crushed
1 carrot, peeled and finely chopped
1 celery stalk, finely chopped
1 zucchini, finely chopped
3¼ cups hot vegetable stock
14oz can of good-quality tomatoes
14oz can of chickpeas
1 teaspoon dried oregano
½ cup orzo
sea salt and freshly ground
    black pepper

Place a large saucepan over medium heat. Pour in the olive oil and then stir in the onion and garlic. Cover and let simmer for 2 minutes.

Stir in the carrot, celery, and zucchini. Cover and let cook for a further 5 minutes.

Pour in the vegetable stock, tomatoes, and chickpeas. Bring to a boil, then reduce the heat and simmer.

Stir in the dried oregano and orzo, season with salt and pepper, and continue to simmer for about 10 minutes or until the orzo is fully cooked and tender.

cook's tip

making soup

- Save your butter wrappers and use them to cover vegetables when sautéeing them to make soup.

- Sauté your vegetables for as long as possible because this intensifies the flavor of the soup.

- Cleaned plastic milk bottles are brilliant for freezing soups in.

pea soup with smoked bacon

The frozen peas in this recipe work brilliantly. They are a staple ingredient that you can have on hand in your freezer in order to make this soup in 20 minutes...

serves 6

pat of butter
1 potato, peeled and diced
1 onion, diced
3 slices of smoked bacon, diced
3¼ cups hot chicken stock
3½ cups frozen peas
generous ⅓ cup heavy cream
sea salt and freshly ground black pepper
2 tablespoons finely chopped fresh mint
scant ¼ cup crème fraîche
a few mint leaves, to garnish

Melt the butter in a heavy-bottomed saucepan over medium heat and add the potato and onion. Reduce the heat, stir, cover, and let sauté for 5 minutes.

Remove the lid, turn the heat up a little, and stir in two-thirds of the bacon. Let cook for a further 3 minutes.

Pour in the chicken stock and let the vegetables simmer for 5 minutes.

Add the frozen peas and cook for 5 minutes.

While the peas are cooking, place a skillet over high heat, add the remaining bacon, and cook for a couple of minutes or until the bacon is nice and crispy. Set aside in a bowl.

Season the soup with salt and pepper, and then purée in a blender.

Stir in the cream and mint.

Pour the hot soup into warmed bowls. Using a teaspoon, add a few drops of crème fraîche to the soup in each bowl, followed by a sprinkle of the fried bacon, and a mint leaf.

Delicious!

cook's tip

making a chill bottle

To keep your smoothies or drinks cold, freeze the carton or plastic bottle overnight. The frozen drink helps keep lunchbox food cool and will have defrosted by lunchtime, leaving you with a lovely refreshing drink.

lip-smacking sandwiches

These are a few of my favorite sandwiches. Wrap them in parchment paper in your lunchbox, or if you are going on a picnic, as I find that plastic wrap can make them a little soggy.

fresh tuna salad

I always feel so healthy after eating this sandwich. If you are trying to cut down on carbs, then don't use any bread and simply eat as a salad instead.

makes 2 rolls

5½oz good-quality canned tuna, drained
½ apple, cored and grated
½ celery stalk, finely sliced
1 tablespoon mayonnaise
grated zest and juice of 1 lemon
sea salt and freshly ground black pepper
2 good-quality whole-wheat rolls
4 leaves of iceberg lettuce (or another
  crispy variety)

Put the tuna, apple, celery, mayonnaise, lemon juice and zest in a bowl. Season with salt and pepper, and mix well.

Cut open the rolls, line them with the lettuce, and scoop the tuna salad mix on top.

smoked salmon with sun-dried tomatoes

It makes such a difference if you use good-quality smoked salmon when making this delicious sandwich.

makes 2 sandwiches

4 teaspoons mayonnaise
4 slices of sourdough bread
10 semi sun-dried tomatoes
12 capers
4 slices of smoked salmon
sea salt and freshly ground black pepper

Spread the mayonnaise over the 4 slices of bread.

Arrange the sun-dried tomatoes and capers on 2 slices of the bread and lay the smoked salmon slices on top.

Season with salt and pepper, and cover with the other 2 slices of bread. Cut in half and enjoy!

new york reuben

Whenever I am in New York City, I go to the famous Katz's Deli and devour one of their amazing Reubens (they do the best in the city). This recipe is the closest I have come to recreating the sandwich in Ireland. The Russian dressing used in this recipe can be made at home or bought in bottles from most good food stores.

makes 2 sandwiches

1 tablespoon grainy Dijon mustard
4 slices rye bread
7oz corned beef, thinly sliced
3½oz Swiss cheese, thinly sliced
7oz sauerkraut, drained
⅛ cup Russian dressing (see below)
⅛ stick butter (optional, for broiling)

For the Russian dressing
⅛ cup mayonnaise
1 teaspoon Worcestershire sauce
1 teaspoon tomato ketchup
1 teaspoon mustard

Spread the mustard on 2 slices of the rye bread. Divide the corned beef between the bread slices, followed by the cheese and sauerkraut. Spread the Russian dressing over the other 2 slices of bread and place on top of the first 2 slices of bread.

You can also broil a Reuben sandwich on a grill pan, which is a more authentic way of making it. Melt the butter on the grill pan. When it has melted, put the prepared sandwiches in the pan and toast both sides.

crispy bacon, creamy avocado, and sweet tomato sambo

Crispy, creamy, sweet, and crunchy—utter heaven in a bite! Make sure you use a good-quality, smoked bacon—I use Gubbeen bacon from a farm in West Cork in Ireland.

makes 2 sandwiches

6 slices of bacon
sunflower oil, for frying
1 ripe avocado, sliced
4 slices of good-quality white bread
8 sweet cherry tomatoes, halved
freshly ground black pepper

Fry the bacon in a drop of sunflower oil in a medium to hot skillet. Cook until the bacon is crispy on both sides. Alternatively, cook under a hot broiler.

Arrange the avocado on 2 slices of bread, followed by the cherry tomatoes and bacon. Season with pepper, cover with the other 2 slices of bread, and cut in half.

asparagus and gruyère tart

The asparagus in this tart is tops for me, but I have also used thinly sliced broccoli and feta instead of the Gruyère, and that combination also works as an absolute treat.

serves 6

For the pastry
½ stick chilled butter, diced
1 cup all-purpose flour
approx. ¼ cup water

For the filling
18 asparagus spears (approx. 10oz)
3 eggs, beaten
¾ cup grated Gruyère
1 cup half and half cream
sea salt and freshly ground black pepper
8 fresh basil leaves

Start by making the pastry. Use your fingertips to rub the butter into the flour, then add enough cold water to bring the pastry dough together. Wrap in plastic wrap and put in the refrigerator to cool for 30 minutes.

Preheat the oven to 350°F.

Once the pastry has chilled, roll it out using a wooden rolling pin and line a 7¾in tart pan, pressing the dough down firmly and trimming off the excess pastry around the edge of the pan. Bake in the oven for 15 minutes.

While the pastry is baking, cook the asparagus by simmering in a small saucepan of salted water for 3 minutes. Drain and slice the spears in half.

Beat together the eggs, cheese, and cream, and season with salt and black pepper.

Pour the egg mixture into the tart and arrange the asparagus spears and fresh basil leaves on top.

Bake the tart at the same temperature for a further 30 minutes or until the center feels firm and looks golden brown.

---

cook's tip

easy pastry rolling

An easy way to roll out your pastry is to place your dough on a sheet of plastic wrap and then lay another one on top. Using your rolling pin, roll out the pastry. The plastic wrap stops the dough from sticking to your countertop and also from breaking up as you roll.

tuscan-style marinated chicken with couscous

The first time that I tasted this recipe was at a wedding on an olive estate in Tuscany. The day after the wedding, they organized a huge barbecue and served this marinated chicken. It's delicious...and I couldn't leave without a copy of the recipe! It works just as well with pork and lamb, too. You might also like to try combining the chicken with my Couscous and Chickpea Salad (see page 42).

serves 4

2 chicken breasts, free range or organic if possible

For the marinade
1 cup olive oil
5 tablespoons balsamic vinegar
1 tablespoon finely chopped rosemary
2 garlic cloves, crushed
sea salt and freshly ground black pepper

For the couscous
1 generous cup couscous
½ cup dried apricots, diced
sea salt and freshly ground black pepper
1½ cups hot chicken stock
2 tablespoons lemon juice
3 tablespoons extra virgin olive oil
⅔ cup slivered almonds, toasted
3⅓ cups baby spinach
⅓ cup feta, crumbled

Place the chicken and all the marinade ingredients in a large bowl and mix well. Cover and put in the refrigerator, and leave to marinate for up to 12 hours.

Preheat the oven to 350°F.

Remove the chicken, place on a hot grill pan, and season with salt and pepper. Cook on each side for 3 minutes before cooking in the oven for 10–15 minutes.

Meanwhile, put the couscous in a large bowl with the apricots, season with salt and black pepper, and mix well. Pour the chicken stock over the couscous and cover immediately with a large plate to seal in the steam. Leave for 10 minutes.

Fluff up the couscous with a fork to separate the grains and stir in the lemon juice, olive oil, almonds, baby spinach, and feta.

Once the chicken is cooked, cut into thin strips, let cool, and fold into the couscous.

couscous and chickpea salad

This is the most popular salad at my Canal Café. It's simple to make, full of fiber, and very low in fat. It will last for about 3 days, so is a great salad to make on a Sunday night for lunch on Monday and Tuesday. It can also be used as a sandwich filler with soft goat cheese.

serves 4

generous 1 cup couscous
¼ cup raisins
1 teaspoon ground cumin
1 teaspoon ground coriander
½ teaspoon ground cinnamon
sea salt and freshly ground black pepper
1½ cups hot chicken stock
½ cup rinsed and drained, good-quality canned chickpeas
2 tablespoons lemon juice
3 tablespoons extra virgin olive oil
¼ red onion, finely diced
2 tablespoons freshly chopped flat-leaf parsley

Put the couscous in a large bowl with the raisins and spices, season with salt and pepper, and mix well. Pour the chicken stock over the couscous and cover immediately with a large plate to seal in the steam. Set aside for 10 minutes.

Fluff up the couscous with a fork to separate the grains and stir in the chickpeas, lemon juice, olive oil, red onion, and parsley.

summer rice salad

This northern Italian salad is super-healthy and often serves as my supper.

serves 2

½ cup rice (basmati or wild)
½ cup frozen peas
¼ cup corn kernels
⅔ cup cherry tomatoes, halved
2 hard-boiled eggs
extra virgin olive oil
juice of 1 lemon
sea salt and freshly ground black pepper

Rinse the rice and put into a saucepan of boiling water. Cook for 15–20 minutes. Rinse again with cold water and let cool.

Place the frozen peas in a saucepan of boiling water and let simmer for 5 minutes, then drain and rinse under cold water. Once the rice has cooled, put it in a large bowl and mix in the corn kernels, peas, and cherry tomatoes.

Cut the hard-boiled eggs into quarters, then halve again, and toss into the rice.

Add some extra virgin olive oil and lemon juice. Season with salt and pepper, and mix well.

banana bread

This delicious recipe can also be used to make muffins. Try adding chopped pecan nuts and walnuts to the recipe. The banana bread will last all week, so is an excellent sweet bread to make for those afternoon treats that we all need!

makes 1 loaf

1 stick butter, plus extra for greasing
¾ cup light soft brown sugar
2 eggs, beaten
3 very ripe bananas, mashed
2 cups all-purpose flour
1 tablespoon baking powder
½ teaspoon grated nutmeg
pinch of sea salt

Preheat the oven to 350°F.

Grease a 2¼lb loaf pan and line the base with parchment paper.

Beat the butter and sugar together until fluffy and pale in color.

Add the eggs, a little at a time, beating well after each addition. Add the bananas to this mixture.

Sift the dry ingredients together and then fold gently into the banana mixture. (It is important to fold the dry ingredients in gently until they are just incorporated, rather than simply stirring.)

Transfer the mixture to the prepared pan and bake for 50–60 minutes or until a skewer placed in the middle of the cake comes out clean and dry.

Turn out onto a wire rack to cool.

peach and honey smoothie

Every day I try to drink a smoothie. I find that it gives me a boost when I am feeling a little bit sluggish...You can use blueberries, strawberries, or raspberries instead of the peaches, if you wish.

makes 1

1 cup fresh peeled and
   sliced peaches
½ banana
2 teaspoons honey
generous ¾ cup plain yogurt
4 ice cubes

Place all the ingredients in a blender and puree until smooth.

oliver's smoothie

Oliver McCabe owns a fabulous food store and café in Ireland called "Select Stores" in Dalkey, County Dublin. His "Ladies" Smoothie is full of the minerals that women need every day, such as calcium, magnesium, and vitamin C. I always feel like I am bursting with energy after his juice; it's fabulous!

makes 2

small bunch of parsley
5 small apples
small bunch of alfalfa sprouts
1 ripe whole mango
1 ripe banana
1 teaspoon organic light tahini
2 teaspoons organic local honey
ice cubes (optional)

Put the parsley and apples in a juicer and juice. Pour the juice into a blender with the rest of the ingredients, then blend for 20 seconds. Add ice if you wish to make the smoothie cooler.

making smoothies

• As fruit tends to deteriorate quite quickly, it is best to freeze berries in bags when you buy them because this also means that you don't have to add in any ice cubes when blitzing.

• If you are trying to cut down on sugar, use honey as an alternative.

• To prevent your blender locking up when making juices or smoothies, add the liquid first and then the solid food.

• If you are freezing smoothies, make sure you leave extra space in your container as they will expand when frozen.

• Mangoes are great for making smoothies sweeter.

crunchy-topped yogurt pots

Yogurt's health credentials are pretty impressive: it boosts the immune system, prevents yeast infections, lowers bad cholesterol, and raises good cholesterol. Because it is rich in calcium, it is good for building bones, and it has been found to have a preventative and curative effect on arthritis. Because it kills the bacteria on your tongue, it can help prevent bad breath. Many people also find it eases ulcers and colitis.

makes 4 yogurt jars

⅓ cup hazelnuts
⅓ cup whole almonds
1¾ cups Greek yogurt
⅓ cup golden raisins
1 teaspoon ground cinnamon

Lightly toast the nuts in a skillet over medium heat for about 3 minutes, tossing every 30 seconds or so to make sure that the nuts are toasted evenly.

Fill the jars three-quarters full with yogurt. Place the toasted nuts, golden raisins, and cinnamon in a bowl and mix well. Spoon the mixture on top of the yogurt.

chocolate and hazelnut drops

I spent two days perfecting this recipe—the cookie crumbles in your mouth and carries just enough chocolate and hazelnuts to make it into the perfect-bite category!

makes 24

2¼ sticks butter, softened
½ cup superfine sugar
2½ cups all-purpose flour
1 teaspoon baking powder
3oz good-quality dark chocolate morsels, minimum 70% cocoa solids
½ cup hazelnuts, roughly chopped

Preheat the oven to 350ºF.

Put the butter and sugar in a large bowl and cream together with a wooden spoon until pale in color.

Sift in the flour and baking powder, and then add the chocolate morsels and hazelnuts. Bring the mixture together to form a dough.

Using your hands, roll the dough into small drops and place them slightly apart on two baking sheets (there is no need to grease or line).

Flatten the drops slightly with the back of a damp fork and bake in the oven for 13–15 minutes or until they are light golden brown and slightly firm on the top.

Carefully transfer the drops to a wire rack to cool.

cook's tip

crushing hazelnuts

Lay a clean dish towel on your countertop, spread out the hazelnuts on the top half of the towel, and cover with the bottom half. Using a rolling pin, forcefully tap the covered hazelnuts. This is an excellent stress-buster, as well as an effective nut-buster!

a guide to cheese

If you're like me, you always keep something in your pantry that you can throw together for a quick meal.

I think of the cheese container in my refrigerator as an extension of the pantry. A good airtight container with a choice of cheeses is an absolute godsend. Cheese is fantastic for quick meals, handy as a snack, and great if people pop round unexpectedly.

I change the cheeses I buy every couple of weeks or so, as there are so many wonderful cheeses to try. I like to take a piece of cheese that I have bought from a local farmers' market or deli when I go out to dinner because people really enjoy hearing about the origins of the cheese.

I prefer to serve cheese with table water crackers because it doesn't detract from the flavor of the cheeses as much. I also serve peeled apples, rather than grapes, to cleanse the palate between cheeses. I also serve chutneys with hard cheese. My Christmas Chutney (see page 18) or my Fig Jam (see page 21) would be superb.

Types of cheese

It's useful to understand the different groups of cheese. If you are offered a cheese board in a restaurant, it should include a hard cheese, a semi-hard cheese, a soft cheese, a fresh cheese, and a blue cheese.

hard cheese (e.g. Cheddar, Parmigiano Reggiano). Good for cooking and lasts for ages. Hard cheese has the highest fat content and can be oily when melted. A good hard cheese has a tangy flavor.

semi-hard cheese (e.g. Gruyère, Emmenthal, Gouda). This lasts about 3–4 weeks in the refrigerator and is good for cooking because it isn't too oily or rubbery.

soft cheese (e.g. Camembert, Brie). This needs to be eaten within a few days of purchase and is best served fully ripe and at room temperature.

fresh cheese (e.g. Ricotta, Mozzarella, Cottage Cheese, Boursin). This is made in two ways: either by curdling milk with an enzyme, draining off the whey, and then molding the remaining curds into cheese or by dropping the curds into hot whey or brine and kneading it, as is the case with mozzarella and burrata.

Fresh cheeses have a reputation for being mild, although this depends on the cheese. For this reason, they often become the vehicle for stronger flavors like herbs or fruits. In fact, they make fantastic, fast, easy meals all on their own. They are also high in protein and calcium, and contain less fat than hard cheese.

Because fresh cheeses don't contain preservatives, they go off quickly and should be eaten as close to the day they were made as possible. When you buy them, there should be no mold and they should smell like fresh milk. Keep them in the refrigerator and stick to the use-by date.

Ricotta and mascarpone are ideal for making trifle or cheesecakes, but they also make a tasty pasta dish added at the last minute with a handful of chopped herbs to a freshly made tomato sauce. Even easier, just add a dollop of ricotta to freshly drained pasta with sautéd mushrooms. Stir in some tarragon and grate over some Irish Desmond or Parmesan cheese. Serve with a crisp white wine and a green salad—a sophisticated meal that won't take you much more than 10 minutes to prepare.

So, let's stop thinking of fresh cheese as something we disguise in casseroles, cakes, and pizza. Don't trifle with it; give it a new lease of life in your main dishes.

blue cheese (e.g. Stilton, Gorgonzola, Cashiel Blue). Veined cheese injected with mold. Works well in salads or with fruit such as pears. Blue cheese is made by milling the curds and thrusting them into molds, which are then hand-turned on a daily basis. After 5 weeks, the cheese goes into a blueing machine, a drumful of spikes then pierce it to let in oxygen, which kickstarts the mold that makes the veins.

using buffalo mozzarella

A popular fresh cheese is mozzarella. If you want to taste the real thing—and trust me you'll never look back—buy Mozzarella di Bufala Campana, a DOP designation (Denomination of Protected Origin) for mozzarella made from buffalo milk produced in Campania, Italy. The texture is not rubbery, but creamy, the flavor is sweet, and it tastes sublime with vine-ripened tomatoes, fresh basil, and a drizzle of olive oil. I also like to tear the mozzarella into pieces and serve it with slices of prosciutto and ripe peaches. Burrata is similar to mozzarella, having both mozzarella and cream inside, which gives it a uniquely soft texture.

recommended goat cheeses

When young, goat cheese is mild and creamy. As it gets older, it hardens and has a sharper, more acidic, taste. Ageing gives cheese depth and intensifies the flavor. You will see goat cheese wrapped in leaves (perhaps soaked in wine or brandy) or rolled in chile or herbs to impart flavor. Goat cheese may also be covered in ash to pull out the moisture. Good goat cheeses include:

From France Crottin de Chavignol, a Pur Chèvre (made only from goat milk) from the Loire is a soft, crumbly cheese, with a slightly nutty flavor, which is at its best at about 4 weeks. Fantastic broiled and served on a green salad with a white wine such as Pouilly Fumé or Sauvignon Blanc.
From Italy Robiola di Roccaverano, a raw or pasteurized cheese made in the provinces of Asti and Alessandria. A soft cheese with no rind and a delicate, slightly sweet taste.
From Spain Cabra del Tietar, a hard cheese with a long nutty finish that is great with Pinot Noir or even sherry.
From England Little Wallop (by Juliet Harbutt and Alex James of Blur) is washed in cider brandy and wrapped in vine leaves. Ready at 3 weeks, it has an appley flavor with a mushroomy aroma and is great with Riesling or Sauvignon Blanc.
From Ireland Bluebell Falls (by Paul Keane) has a creamy, nutty, caramel flavor that can hold its own with any of the great pecorino cheeses. Try with a Sauvignon Blanc or even a Pinot Noir.

food for family and friends

sweet, sticky, and devilishly good

a breakfast frittata cooked in one skillet couldn't be simpler.

homemade beans on hot buttered toast must be the ultimate comfort food.

decorating with flowers

It's a wet Dublin day. I open my sitting-room door to be wowed by a splash of sunshine in a vase: my daffodils have opened overnight. They are so vibrant, so impossibly pretty that I can't help but feel happy. Now, those daffodils only cost a few dollars; that's a disproportionate amount of pleasure for so little cost. Freshly cut flowers are like the smell of fresh coffee or baking bread. They turn the house into a home. They are also a great way to express yourself, so be creative and use whatever you have around you.

Any watertight container works as a vase. I use mismatched containers such as medicine jars or old milk bottles with my vases, but use one type of flower throughout the house. It makes more of a statement. Also, if you're given a large bunch of one type of flowers, break them up and display them in a row rather than putting them all in one vase. It has more impact, particularly with large blooms like chrysanthemums.

I also have a ribbon drawer where I save ties and bows from presents or chocolates. I tie them around vases for an extra dash of color or to add a touch of zing to the display. A final word: buy flowers when they are in season. It's when they're at their most beautiful and gives us something new to look forward to as the seasons change.

the lazy brunch

Weekdays, I'm usually rushing out of the door with a slice of toast and a cell phone clamped to my ear. So, when it comes to the weekend, there is nothing I like more than waking up when I'm ready and having a lazy brunch.

I love the relaxed informality and flexibility of brunch. It can take place any time from mid-morning to mid-afternoon. When I was at college in the United States, I picked up some great tips on lazy, laid-back brunches. Serving brunch buffet-style, for example, means that you don't have to be a short-order cook and can offer plenty of variety. You can't go wrong with a classic egg dish such as Eggs Florentine, while pancakes and muffins are easy to prepare ahead of time and always popular. I also like to serve something sweet. My favorite sweet dish is Cinnamon French Toast with Honey-Vanilla Mascarpone.

Ideally, a brunch stretches itself out over a few hours, so there is time for fruit juice and coffee first. Drinks are vital: the coffee has to be good-quality, the fruit juices fresh, and any alcohol chilled. After a hectic week, brunch is a casual affair, preferably eaten in your pyjamas. The only brunch rule is that there are no rules—just sit back, enjoy your coffee, and keep it coming!

croque madame

My favorite place to eat Croque Madame or Monsieur (the difference being that the Monsieur is a closed sandwich while the Madame is open-faced) is in Café de Flore in St. Germain, in Paris. It's a very simple, bistro-style café where the great artists and writers of Paris would come to share their thoughts.

serves 2

4 slices of sourdough white bread
1 tablespoon butter
2 slices of cooked ham
1 tablespoon Dijon mustard
6 tablespoons grated Gruyère
sea salt and freshly ground black pepper

cook's tip

a perfect poached egg

There is a very simple trick to this—make sure that your water is salted and on a rolling boil. Then, with a spoon, swirl the water and crack the egg as close to the water as possible (without burning your fingers). You will instantly see the white of the egg cover the yolk. You must also make sure that the eggs are fresh.

Place the sliced bread under a broiler and toast one side. Remove from the broiler and butter the non-toasted side.

Place half a slice of ham and a smear of Dijon mustard on each slice of bread.

Top with equal amounts of grated Gruyère, then season with salt and pepper.

Put back underneath the broiler until the cheese has melted.

cook's tip

a perfect boiled egg

Add a little sprinkle of salt to the water and make sure that the water is boiling and covers the egg by an inch. Then the timings! You will need to boil your egg for 3 minutes for a really soft-boiled yolk, 4 minutes for a slightly set yolk, 5 minutes for a firmer yolk, 6 minutes for hard-boiled with a slightly soft yolk, and 8 minutes for firmly hard-boiled.

classic eggs florentine

Every time I visit New York City, I eat a Sunday brunch at Balthazar. Their Eggs Florentine are so good; they serve the dish with sliced artichokes as well as spinach. Hollandaise is usually a tricky sauce to make because it can split, but try my way of making it in a food processor, and I promise you that it will be absolute perfection!

serves 2

sunflower oil, for frying
4 slices of smoked bacon
4 free range or organic eggs
½ stick butter
5 cups spinach, stalks removed

For the Hollandaise sauce
scant ½ cup butter
2 egg yolks
juice of 1 lemon
sea salt and freshly ground
 black pepper

Place a skillet over a medium heat, add a drop of oil, and fry off the bacon until it is golden brown and crispy. Once cooked, place in a low-heated oven to keep warm.

To make the Hollandaise sauce, first melt the butter in a saucepan. While the butter is melting, pour the egg yolks into a food processor, followed by the lemon juice. Turn on the food processor to a medium speed, and slowly pour the melted butter through the feed tube until the butter and egg yolks are thoroughly combined and the sauce has a thick consistency. Season with salt and pepper.

For the poached eggs, place a saucepan of salted water over high heat and, once the water has come to a boil, give the water a good swirl with a spoon. (Swirling the water helps the white of the egg to form around the yolk.) Bring the eggs, one at a time, as close to the boiling water as possible and crack quite quickly into the water. Reduce the heat to medium and let cook for 3 minutes.

While the eggs are poaching, place a skillet over high heat and melt the butter. Stir in the spinach and cook until the leaves are wilted.

Arrange the wilted spinach on 2 warmed plates. Place 2 poached eggs on each plate. Pour over the Hollandaise sauce and place the smoked bacon on top. Serve with toast.

full breakfast frittata

This recipe is just superb for when you are cooking brunch for a large number. It will take you about 20 minutes to prepare, but once it is cooked, it can be left to sit in a preheated oven while you get the coffee made.

serves 4

8 free range or organic eggs
sea salt and freshly ground
  black pepper
4 tablespoons olive oil
1 onion, sliced
1 cup peeled and diced potato
4 sausages, cut into ⅜in slices
½ cup smoked thick-cut bacon, diced
8 cherry tomatoes, halved

Crack the eggs into a large bowl, season with salt and pepper, and whisk lightly.

Place a 12in skillet over medium heat and pour in 3 tablespoons of the olive oil. When the oil is hot, add the onion and potatoes, reduce the heat, and let cook for 10 minutes, stirring every few minutes.

Once the potatoes and onion are cooked, add them to the bowl of whisked eggs, season with salt and pepper, and mix together.

Place the skillet back on a low heat, add another tablespoon of olive oil, tip in the sausages and bacon lardons, and cook for 5 minutes. Add to the egg mixture.

Put the skillet back on the heat and, if necessary, pour in a small amount of olive oil. Pour in the egg mixture. Let cook for about 10 minutes or until the egg mixture has set.

Arrange the halved cherry tomatoes on top.

Put the frittata under the broiler for 5 minutes or until it is golden in color.

···· cook's tip ····

tempting alternatives

Try substituting the smoked bacon and sausages for smoked salmon and soft goat or ricotta cheese. I've also made a delicious Spanish version using chorizo and manchego cheese.

baked eggs

This must be the most simple and scrumptious way to cook eggs. When baking the eggs, make sure that you bake only one or two in a dish at a time because the eggs on the outside get overcooked if you cook more than that.

serves 2

¼ stick butter
4 free range or organic eggs
½ cup Gruyère cheese (or another hard cheese such as Cheddar or Gouda), grated
1 teaspoon mustard
1 tablespoon heavy cream
sea salt and freshly ground black pepper
slices of bread, to serve

Preheat the oven to 350°F.

Grease 2 small ovenproof dishes with the butter and crack 2 eggs into each one.

Put the cheese in a small bowl and mix in the mustard and cream. Season with salt and pepper. Scoop the cheese mixture on top of the eggs and bake in the oven for 10 minutes.

Serve with toasted bread cut into thin slices so that you can dip them into the eggs.

variations

Add ⅓ cup of diced, smoked thick-cut bacon to the cheese mixture.

Omit the cream mixture and place 4 thin slices of spicy chorizo on top of the eggs.

Wilt 2 cups of baby spinach in a skillet with some butter, and bed the dishes with the spinach before you crack in the eggs.

Try sprinkling some bread crumbs on top of the cheese mixture to get a nice crispy finish.

----- cook's tip -----

keep it fresh

You can test to see if an egg is fresh by dropping it into a bowl of cold water. If the egg stays at the bottom of the bowl, then it is fresh.

homemade beans on toast

3 shallots, thinly sliced
1 garlic clove, crushed
olive oil, for frying
¾ cup tomato sauce
2 tablespoons cider vinegar
1 tablespoon corn syrup
  or dark muscovado sugar
sea salt and freshly ground black pepper
3¼ cups cooked cannellini beans

Homemade beans are best made the day before. I also love adding two teaspoons of medium curry powder. They will last in the refrigerator for 1 week after you make them.

serves 4

Put the shallots and garlic in a flameproof Dutch oven over medium heat and sauté in a drop of olive oil for 2–3 minutes.

Stir in the tomato sauce, vinegar, and syrup (or sugar), season with salt and pepper, and let simmer for 5 minutes.

Stir the cannellini beans into the tomato mixture, cover, and let cook for 70–80 minutes, stirring occasionally. Serve on hot buttered toast.

macedonian fruit salad

2 bananas
1 peach
1 apple
1 kiwifruit
1 orange
10 grapes
¾ cup + 2 tablespoons water
juice of 1 lemon
1 teaspoon superfine sugar (optional)

Even though I have put this fruit salad in the brunch section, it's a fabulous recipe to make for snacking through the day too. I picked up this recipe while living in Italy.

serves 4

Peel and slice all of the fruit and place in a large bowl. Pour in the water and lemon juice, and mix well. Have a taste; if all the fruit is ripe, you shouldn't have to add any sugar, but sprinkle over some superfine sugar if it's lacking in sweetness.

Cover and put in the refrigerator to marinate for an hour before serving.

cinnamon french toast with honey-vanilla mascarpone

French toast is my all-time favorite brunch dish, especially when it is made with brioche. If you don't have any brioche, then just use good-quality white bread. If you aren't a fan of cinnamon, then try some freshly grated nutmeg. At my café, we also serve this with crispy bacon.

makes 4

For the French toast
⅔ cup milk
4 eggs
2 teaspoons ground cinnamon
8 slices of brioche
¼ stick butter

For the honey-vanilla mascarpone cream
¾ cup + 2 tablespoons mascarpone
2 tablespoons honey
½ teaspoon vanilla extract

Put the milk, eggs, and cinnamon in a bowl and beat well. Soak the brioche slices in the milk-and-egg mixture for a couple of minutes.

While the slices of brioche are soaking, put the mascarpone, honey, and vanilla extract in a bowl, and mix together well.

Melt the butter in a skillet and fry the egg-soaked slices of brioche over medium heat until they are a golden color on each side.

Serve the French toast with a spoonful of the mascarpone cream.

new-york-style blueberry pancakes

These pancakes are great for serving when you have children to feed for brunch, as they all love pancakes. You can substitute the blueberries with raspberries or chocolate morsels if you wish. Make the batter the night before, so your brunch can remain as relaxed as possible...

makes 10 pancakes

1¼ cups self-rising flour
1 tablespoon baking powder
¼ cup superfine sugar
1 egg
1¼ cups milk
1 stick butter (½ stick melted)
1¾ cups fresh blueberries
maple syrup, to serve

To make the pancake batter, sift the flour, baking powder, and sugar into a large bowl.

In a separate bowl, whisk the egg and milk together.

Make a well in the center of the flour mixture, pour in the milk-and-egg mixture and whisk together until you have a smooth creamy consistency. Place in the refrigerator for a minimum of 1 hour.

Just before cooking the pancakes, stir in the melted butter (or a tablespoon of vegetable oil), which prevents the pancakes from sticking to the pan, and the fresh blueberries.

Over a medium heat, melt a pat of butter in a 12in nonstick skillet, making sure that the butter spreads out all over the base of the pan to form a film.

Spoon 4 tablespoons of batter into the pan. You should be able to fit 3 pancakes at a time on the pan, but remember to leave space in between each one. When you see bubbles forming on the surface of the batter, turn over the pancake and continue to cook on the other side until it is a light golden color.

As you make them, put the cooked pancakes onto a warm plate covered with foil in a low-heated oven.

When you have cooked all of your pancakes, place them on a warmed plate and serve with the maple syrup.

very berry muffins

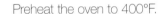

I make these muffins with buttermilk as I think it adds more flavor, but you can also use normal milk.

makes 12 muffins

3¼ cups all-purpose flour
¾ cup superfine sugar
1 tablespoon baking powder
finely grated zest of 1 orange
pinch of sea salt
1 cup + 2 tablespoons buttermilk
2 eggs, beaten
¾ stick butter, melted
1¾ cups blackberries or blueberries, or
  2 cups raspberries

Preheat the oven to 400°F.

Grease a 12-cup muffin pan and set aside.

Mix the flour, sugar, baking powder, orange zest, and salt in a large bowl.

In a separate bowl, mix together the buttermilk, eggs, and melted butter. Make a well in the center of the flour mixture and pour in the buttermilk mixture, mixing all the time until the mixture is quite stiff.

Fold in the berries of your choice and fill the muffin cups with the mixture.

Bake in the oven for 15 minutes. Remove from the oven once the muffins have risen and are a golden color on top. Turn out onto a wire rack and let cool.

cook's tip

other muffin ideas

To make chocolate muffins, substitute the berries with 5½oz of good-quality dark chocolate morsels. For cranberry muffins, substitute the berries with 1¾ cups of dried cranberries.

homemade muesli

I usually prepare five times the quantity of this recipe when I am making muesli and then store it in large airtight jars. It's fabulous in the morning sprinkled over yogurt or oatmeal. You can also try adding a teaspoon of ground cinnamon.

makes 12 servings

3 cups rolled oats
¾ cup dried figs
¾ cup dried apricot halves
½ cup dried cranberries
1½ cups mixed nuts
   (almonds, hazelnuts, walnuts)
⅓ cup pumpkin seeds
⅓ cup sunflower seeds

Preheat the oven to 375°F.

Spread out the oats over the base of a large roasting pan and roast in the oven for 15 minutes or until golden in color. Put the roasted oats in a large bowl and let cool.

Roughly chop the dried fruits and nuts. Put the seeds and chopped fruits and nuts in the bowl. Mix well.

Transfer to an airtight container and serve for breakfast with some plain yogurt or milk.

pecan swirls

Sweet, sticky, and devilishly good—just make sure that you make enough of these swirls for everyone, as they tend to disappear very fast!

makes 16

For the dough
3½ cups all-purpose flour
¼ cup superfine sugar
1 teaspoon sea salt
¾ stick chilled unsalted butter, diced
½oz fresh yeast
⅔ cup milk
2 eggs

For the filling
1 cup pecan halves
scant ½ cup brown sugar
2 teaspoons ground cinnamon
a little melted butter for brushing

For the topping
1 cup pecan halves, chopped
1 stick butter, melted
¼ cup brown sugar
⅓ cup maple syrup

Put the flour, sugar, and salt in a large bowl and rub in the butter with your fingertips until the mixture resembles bread crumbs.

Activate the yeast by mixing in a sprinkle of superfine sugar using the back of a teaspoon until the yeast becomes liquidy. Whisk the yeast into the milk, followed by the eggs, and then pour the milk mixture into the dry ingredients. Mix well.

Place the dough onto a lightly floured board and knead for 10–15 minutes. Put the dough in a lightly oiled bowl, cover with plastic wrap (or a cloth) and place in a warm dry place (such as a rack above a stove) for an hour.

Make the filling by putting the pecans, sugar, and cinnamon into a food processor and grinding until the ingredients are finely ground.

Once the dough has been rising for an hour, knead it for a further 5 minutes. Cut the dough into two and roll and stretch each piece on a lightly floured board until it measures about 10 x 14in.

Brush some melted butter over the two pieces of dough. Sprinkle half the filling over each rectangle, then use a rolling pin to press it into the dough. Then, tightly roll each rectangle, starting at a long side, in order to create a jelly-roll-like shape. Cut each log into 8 pieces (about ¾in thick) and put the swirls into 2 deep baking sheets.

Make the topping by mixing together the pecans, melted butter, sugar, and syrup. Brush each side of the swirl slices with the mixture. Cover and place in a warm dry spot for a further 30 minutes. Make sure that you leave enough space between each of the swirls to let them rise and expand.

Preheat the oven to 375°F. Once the swirls have risen, bake in the oven for 20 minutes. Let cool before eating (if you can!).

the lazy brunch

bloody mary

I adore having a Bloody Mary with brunch, especially after a late night out! Leave out the vodka to make a Virgin Mary.

makes 1

2 shots of vodka (about 2 capfuls)
juice of ½ lemon
5 dashes Worcestershire sauce
3 dashes Tabasco sauce
¾ cup tomato juice
pinch of sea salt and freshly ground
  black pepper
1 celery stalk, to serve

Pour the vodka, lemon juice, Worcestershire sauce, Tabasco sauce, and tomato juice into a glass, season with salt and pepper, and mix well with a spoon.

Serve with a stalk of celery and 3 ice cubes in each glass.

---

cook's tip

brunch-time cocktails

To make a Bellini, take 3 ripe peaches (peeled and pitted), put them in a food processor and purée. Divide the peach purée between 6 champagne flutes, top up with champagne or sparkling wine, and stir.

To make a Mimosa, take 2 cups of fresh orange juice and chill. Just before serving, fill 6 champagne glasses with one-third orange juice and the rest of the glass with champagne or sparkling wine.

the relaxed sunday lunch

Sunday is the most perfect time to gather friends and family around for a little feast. Get everyone involved in the cooking and in setting the table. Food served in big dishes is the way to go so that no one feels stressed.

Sunday lunch is all about getting together at a relaxed, convivial table. A delicious roast, seasonal vegetables, and a heavenly dessert are what the Sunday lunch table calls for. Once you have roasted your choice of meat, you can make the perfect gravy to accompany it by placing the roasting pan over a moderate heat to loosen the juices; this will take approximately 2–3 minutes. Scrape at the bits stuck to the base of the pan (they contain lots of delicious flavors), then pour in some stock, whisking as you do so. You can also add some red wine or cream at this stage, too. Strain the gravy through a sieve before you serve.

Everyone loves roast potatoes served with a roast. To make perfect roast potatoes, peel the potatoes, then boil them for approximately 10 minutes. Drain the potatoes, toss in olive oil (or goose fat!), season with sea salt and freshly ground black pepper, and roast in a moderate oven for 30 minutes, giving them a toss every 5 minutes. For an Italian alternative, crush the roast potatoes when cooked and mix in some finely chopped black olives.

pine nut and rosemary crusted lamb

I love the crunchy crust on this lamb dish. You could also use thyme instead of the rosemary. I have often used this recipe for a leg of lamb and it works perfectly.

serves 4

½ cup pine nuts, roughly chopped
2 tablespoons roughly chopped fresh rosemary
1 garlic clove, crushed
½ stick butter, melted
4 x 2–3 cutlet racks of lamb, trimmed
sea salt and freshly ground black pepper

Preheat the oven to 350°F.

Put the pine nuts, fresh rosemary, and garlic in a bowl and pour over the melted butter. Mix and set aside.

Heat a skillet and seal the racks of lamb on all sides. Place the racks of lamb in an ovenproof dish. Spread the pine nut and rosemary topping over the lamb.

Roast the lamb in the oven for 10–15 minutes for medium and a further 5–10 minutes for well done.

Take out of the oven, loosely cover with foil, and let rest for 10 minutes before serving.

roasting times

beef and lamb

475°F for 15 mins, then 400°F

for rare
cook for 10 mins per 18oz

for medium
cook for 14 mins per 18oz

for well done
cook for 16–18 mins per 18oz

chicken

425°F for 15 mins, then 375°F

Cook for 20 mins per 18oz

pork

425°F for 20 minutes, then 350°F

Cook for 20 mins per 18oz

moroccan-spiced roast chicken

This spice mixture is also great for marinating a fillet of chicken breast for the grill or broiling in the kitchen. Simply add more olive oil so that it's more liquidy. I like to carve the chicken before I bring it to the table, and lay it all out on a large warmed platter that is bedded with some delicious spicy couscous.

serves 4

2 teaspoons ground cumin
1 teaspoon ground coriander
1 teaspoon mild chile powder
1 teaspoon paprika
½ teaspoon ground cinnamon
2 garlic cloves, crushed
2 tablespoons lemon juice
2 tablespoons olive oil
3lb 5oz free-range or organic chicken
sea salt and freshly ground black pepper

Preheat the oven to 350°F.

Put all the spices, garlic, lemon juice, and olive oil in a bowl and mix well together.

Rinse the chicken under cold water and pat dry with paper towels.

Smear the spice mixture under the skin of the chicken, using a spoon or clean hands. This makes a world of difference to the final taste as the spices get right into the meat of the chicken.

Put the chicken in a baking dish. Place the lemon halves that you juiced earlier into the cavity of the chicken. Season the chicken with salt and pepper and place in the oven for 70 minutes.

Baste the chicken by spooning the cooking juices from the bottom of the baking dish over the chicken every 20 minutes.

To test if the chicken is cooked, pierce with a skewer (or a sharp knife). If the juices run clear, the chicken is cooked; if they are still pink, leave the chicken to cook for a further 10 minutes, and then test again.

Serve with my Couscous and Chickpea Salad (see page 42).

ways to roast a chicken

For all the following recipes, you will need 1 chicken (approx. 5lb in weight). Once prepared, put the chicken in a preheated oven at 350°F for 90 minutes.

paprika, garlic, and lemon spiced chicken

to make: Put 1 garlic clove (crushed) in a bowl, whisk in the juice of 1 lemon, ⅓ cup of olive oil, and 2 teaspoons of paprika, season with sea salt and freshly ground black pepper, and blend. Lift the flap of skin at the rear of the chicken and smear some of the spiced oil all over the meat under the skin. Rub the rest of the oil over the legs and wings.

serve with: Lemon and Thyme Roasties (page 87)

tarragon, white wine, and garlic butter

to make: Place a saucepan over low heat and pour in 1 tablespoon of olive oil. Stir in 2 shallots (finely diced) and 2 garlic cloves (crushed), and cook for 1 minute. Pour in generous ⅓ cup of white wine and let cook for a further 3–4 minutes until the wine reduces. Take the pan off the heat and let cool. Place ½ stick of softened butter and 2 teaspoons of fresh tarragon in a bowl, add the shallots and garlic, and season with sea salt and freshly ground black pepper. Use the back of a spoon to blend everything together. Lift the flap of skin at the rear of the chicken and smear some of the butter all over the meat under the skin. Rub the rest of the butter over the legs and wings.

serve with: Celeriac and Potato Gratin (page 85)

indian-spiced roast chicken

to make: Grind together 1 teaspoon of fresh ginger, 1 garlic clove, ½ teaspoon of ground coriander, 1 clove, a pinch of turmeric, 1 green chile, and 2 tablespoons of water until you have a thick paste. Mix 2 tablespoons of Greek yogurt and 2 teaspoons of lemon juice with the spice mix, season with sea salt and freshly ground black pepper, and blend. Lift the flap of skin at the rear of the chicken and smear some of the yogurt mix all over the meat under the skin. Rub the rest of the yogurt mix over the legs and wings.

serve with: Fresh Raita (page 176)

thai-style roast chicken

to make: Put 1 stick of lemongrass, 2 garlic cloves, ½ can of coconut milk, 2 teaspoons of fresh ginger, 2 tablespoons of fish sauce, 2 tablespoons of soy sauce, the juice of 1 lime, and 2 sprigs of fresh cilantro in a food processor, season with salt and freshly ground black pepper, and blend. Lift the flap of skin at the rear of the chicken and smear some of the mix all over the meat under the skin. Rub the rest of the mix over the legs and wings.

serve with: Jasmine Rice

spiced apple pork loin

The spicy apple flavors oozing their way into the pork loin make for the most delicious roast pork, while the juices in the pan are sublime! After you have carved the pork loin, pour over the spicy apple juice from the pan. I particularly love this dish served with gratin Dauphinoise potatoes.

serves 4

½ stick butter
7oz apples (variety suitable for cooking), diced
1 onion, diced
½ cup brown sugar
4 cloves
1 teaspoon medium chile powder
1 teaspoon turmeric powder
1 in piece of fresh ginger,
   peeled and finely chopped
¼ cup + 2 tablespoons cider vinegar
sea salt and freshly ground
   black pepper
4lb 8oz pork loin

Preheat the oven to 400°F.

Melt the butter in a saucepan over medium heat and add the apples and onion. Cook for 10 minutes, and then stir in the brown sugar, cloves, chile powder, turmeric powder, fresh ginger, and cider vinegar. Season with salt and pepper. Mix well.

Cover the saucepan and let simmer over a medium heat for 10 minutes. Take the lid off, turn down the heat, and let cook for a further 5 minutes or until the apple has broken down and turned a rich golden brown color.

Place the pork loin in a large roasting pan and pour the spiced apple mixture all over the meat.

Roast in the oven for 1½ hours, basting the pork with the cooking juices from the bottom of the pan every 20 minutes.

beef rib roast with creamy black pepper gravy

It's definitely worth making a trip to a good butcher to pick out a good rib of beef. The meat should be a dark brownish color and not bright red. The darker color means that it has been hung for longer and will therefore be more tender. Also, a thin marbling of fat all over the meat is something else to look out for because this means that the flavors from the fat will be dispersed throughout the meat.

serves 6

6lb 8oz bone-in beef rib roast
bunch of fresh rosemary
2 garlic cloves, thinly sliced
1 teaspoon sea salt
1 teaspoon freshly ground
   black pepper
2 teaspoons olive oil

For the gravy
1¾ cups light cream
1 teaspoon Dijon mustard
2 teaspoons freshly ground
   black pepper, plus a little extra
   for seasoning

Bring the beef up to room temperature by taking it out of the refrigerator 30 minutes before cooking and let it rest on the kitchen counter. This is important, as a cold piece of meat going into the oven will not be as tender.

Preheat the oven to 425°F.

Using a knife, make 6 slits in the beef and push a sprig of rosemary and a thin slice of garlic into the slits. Rub the sea salt and black pepper into the meat.

Place a roasting pan over medium heat and add the olive oil. When the oil is hot, sear the meat on all sides until it is brown. Roast the beef in the oven for 20 minutes, then reduce the oven temperature to 325°F and continue to cook for 20 minutes per 1lb of beef for medium or 15 minutes per 1lb for rare.

When the beef is cooked, transfer to a serving dish, cover with foil and let rest for 30 minutes before carving. This will allow the meat to relax and tenderize.

Place the roasting pan over a warm stovetop and pour in the cream, mustard, and black pepper. With a whisk gather all the delicious juices from the beef and mix in with the cream. The creamy gravy will begin to thicken after a couple of minutes.

Serve the gravy hot with the beef.

cook's tip

roast parsnips and carrots

Peel and cut 6 parsnips and 6 carrots into wedges. Place the vegetables in a roasting pan and put the meat that you are roasting on top. All the gorgeous juices from the meat will trickle down into the vegetables, making the best roast vegetables ever!

spring ratatouille

The great thing about making a large pan of ratatouille is that you can use some of it the following week, perhaps served with couscous, folded through pasta, or in sandwiches with some goat cheese.

serves 6

1 eggplant
1 zucchini
1 red bell pepper, seeded
1 yellow bell pepper, seeded
1 garlic clove, crushed
14oz canned chopped tomatoes
sea salt and freshly ground
  black pepper
olive oil
bunch of fresh basil

Preheat the oven to 350°F.

Slice the eggplant, zucchini, and bell peppers into wedges.

Put the vegetables, garlic, and tomatoes in a baking dish, season with salt and pepper, add some olive oil and mix well.

Bake in the oven for 30 minutes or until the vegetables are tender.

Stir in the fresh basil leaves just before serving.

celeriac and potato gratin

I love the aniseed flavor of celeriac. If you're not a huge fan of aniseed, just omit the celeriac and use all potato. You can also grate some Gruyère or Fontina cheese in between the layers.

serves 6

¾ stick butter, softened,
    plus a little extra for greasing
1 garlic clove, crushed
2lb potatoes, peeled and thinly sliced
18oz celeriac, peeled, cut into quarters,
    and thinly sliced
sea salt and freshly ground black pepper
2 cups half and half
¼ teaspoon freshly grated nutmeg

Preheat the oven to 350°F.

Grease a baking dish with butter and sprinkle the crushed garlic on the bottom of the dish.

Drop the sliced potatoes and celeriac into a saucepan of boiling water for 4–5 minutes, then drain and make layers in the dish, overlapping the slices a little and seasoning each layer.

Pour the half and half over the potatoes and use your hand to push down the potatoes until they are completely immersed in the milk. Sprinkle the nutmeg over the potatoes and cover with a butter wrapper.

Bake in the oven for 30 minutes. Remove the butter wrapper and turn up the heat to 400°F until the top is golden (about 20 minutes).

summer garden salad

This salad is so refreshing served with a roast. It's important that the vegetables are cut into thin cruditées. I would usually make this salad a couple of hours before lunch so that the oil, mustard, and vinegar have a chance to infuse the vegetables.

serves 4

3 carrots
1 fennel bulb
1 cucumber
3 radishes
1 teaspoon Dijon mustard
6 tablespoons extra virgin olive oil
2 tablespoons white wine vinegar
sea salt and freshly ground black pepper
½ cup toasted pine nuts

Slice all the vegetables into thin cruditée sticks and place in a large serving bowl.

Whisk the mustard, olive oil, and vinegar in a small bowl and season with salt and pepper.

Toss the vegetables in the dressing and sprinkle over the pine nuts.

spicy sweet potato fries

Sweet potatoes make such great fries, just be careful not to overcook them, as they can go very mushy. Delicious served with crème fraîche...

serves 6

1 teaspoon ground cumin
2 tablespoons olive oil
sea salt and freshly ground black pepper
2¼lb sweet potatoes, peeled

Preheat the oven to 400°F.

In a small bowl, mix together the ground cumin and olive oil, season with salt and pepper and set aside.

Cut the sweet potatoes in half lengthwise and cut each half into 6 wedges (fat fries!).

In a large bowl, mix together the potatoes and spiced oil mixture. Toss until the potatoes are evenly coated.

Arrange the potato fries in a roasting pan and roast in the oven for 35–40 minutes or until the edges are crisp and the potatoes are cooked through.

lemon and thyme roasties

The lemon juice in this dish adds a delicious zestiness to these roast potatoes. Rosemary is also a fabulous alternative to the thyme.

serves 6

1 ¼lb potatoes (a floury variety)
juice and skin of 1 lemon
½ cup + 2 tablespoons olive oil
4 sprigs of fresh thyme
2 garlic cloves
sea salt and freshly ground black pepper

Preheat the oven to 350°F.

Wash and peel the potatoes. Chop the potatoes into small cubes and place in a pot of simmering salted water for 5 minutes, then drain and place in a large bowl.

Pour the juice of the lemon and the olive oil onto the potatoes. Sprinkle the thyme into the bowl, add the garlic, season with salt and pepper, and mix well.

Chop up the lemon skins that you juiced and add to the potatoes for extra flavor.

Transfer the potatoes to a baking dish and roast in the oven for 20 minutes, tossing them every 10 minutes so that they are thoroughly coated with all of the flavors.

Before serving, remove the lemon skins and whole garlic cloves.

italian rosemary crispbreads

I serve these crispbreads with our salad plates at my café. They are so simple to make and are fabulous stacked in the middle of the table for people to nibble on.

makes 8

⅓ cup warm water
¼ teaspoon dried yeast
scant 1¾ cups all-purpose flour
2 tablespoons olive oil
sea salt
1 egg
3 sprigs of fresh rosemary, finely chopped

Preheat the oven to 350°F.

Pour the water into a bowl and sprinkle in the dried yeast. Allow the yeast to foam, which should take about 5 minutes.

Put the flour in a large bowl, pour the yeast mixture on top, and add the olive oil and a sprinkle of sea salt. Stir together until a dough forms.

Turn the dough out onto a floured counter and knead for 10 minutes. Transfer to an oiled bowl, cover with a dish towel, and place in a warm dry spot for an hour.

Divide the dough into 8 pieces and roll each piece to roughly 10 x 4in on a lightly floured counter.

Transfer to a baking sheet that has been lined with parchment paper. Brush with egg wash (using 1 egg and a splash of water whisked together), sprinkle with sea salt and fresh rosemary. Repeat with the remaining dough.

Bake in the oven for 20 minutes or until crisp and golden. Let cool on wire racks.

variation
Try adding some finely chopped black olives or sun-dried tomatoes to the recipe.

cook's tip

lovely gift ideas

These crispbreads also make a fabulous gift if you are visiting a friend's house for supper. Simply wrap them in parchment paper, tie with twine, and stick a sprig of rosemary in the knot.

baked cauliflower cheese

This is pure comfort food...Sometimes, I use Gruyère instead of the Cheddar because it gives the dish a more nutty flavor. It's also a great dish to serve when you have to feed lots of people for lunch.

serves 4

1 small cauliflower
¾ stick butter
scant ¾ cup all-purpose flour
1¾ cups milk
7 cups grated mature Cheddar cheese
pinch of freshly ground black pepper

Preheat the oven to 350°F.

Remove the outer leaves from the cauliflower and chop them coarsely.

Place the whole cauliflower and the chopped leaves in a saucepan with about 1in of water. Cook over medium heat for 10 minutes (you want the cauliflower florets to be slightly undercooked because they will be going in the oven too).

In a separate saucepan, make the cheese sauce by melting the butter and whisking in the flour. Cook for 2–3 minutes, stirring constantly. Add the milk gradually, whisking continuously to ensure that no lumps form. Stir in the grated cheese and pepper.

Place the cauliflower in a lightly buttered gratin dish and pour over the cheese sauce. Bake in the oven for 20 minutes and serve immediately.

the relaxed sunday lunch

creamed spinach with nutmeg

The great thing about this recipe is that it acts as both a sauce and a vegetable. It's delicious served with lamb, beef, and chicken.

serves 4

¼ stick butter
16¾ cups baby spinach
¾ cup + 2 tablespoons half and half
pinch of freshly grated nutmeg
sea salt and freshly ground black pepper

Melt the butter in a large skillet over high heat, then add in the baby spinach and cook for 2 minutes.

Pour the half and half over the spinach and let cook for 5 minutes (you will see the cream thickening).

Scatter the nutmeg over and season with salt and pepper. Transfer to a warm serving bowl and serve.

variation
Try substituting the spinach with finely sliced mushrooms.

roasted artichokes with lemon thyme

This is absolutely delicious served on a piece of bruschetta (which is toasted sourdough with a drizzle of olive oil), mixed in a salad, or just on its own for an appetizer with a lemon mayonnaise.

serves 2

6 artichoke hearts, boiled
juice of 1 lemon
olive oil
1 teaspoon finely chopped fresh thyme
sea salt and freshly ground black pepper

Preheat the oven to 350°F.

Slice the cooked artichoke hearts into quarters and place on a baking sheet. Drizzle with the lemon juice and some olive oil.

Sprinkle with the fresh thyme and season with salt and pepper. Mix well.

Bake in the oven for 10 minutes—and that's it!

············ cook's tip ············

preparing and cooking an artichoke

Firstly, snap off the stalk and cut off the pointed tips of the leaves with a pair of scissors. You can cook the artichoke in two ways. If you're cooking the artichoke whole, simmer in boiling water with the juice of one lemon for about 30 minutes, and then just pull away the leaves. If you simply want to use the heart, prise open the leaves from the top of the artichoke until you come to the hairy choke (heart). Tear the heart out and scoop away any fibers at the base with a teaspoon, and then you can either roast or boil the heart. The choke discolors very quickly, so keep it in a bowl of water with a few slices of lemon.

baked ricotta cake

This cake is fantastic because it lasts for 10 days and the flavor gets better as the days go by. Well, that's if it has a chance to...!

serves 10

1¾ cups ricotta
4 eggs, separated
2 tablespoons all-purpose flour
grated zest and juice of 2 lemons
scant 1 cup superfine sugar
scant ½ cup (just over ½ stick) butter
12 graham crackers, crushed

Preheat the oven to 350°F.

Place the ricotta in a bowl and mix in the yolks of the eggs, followed by the flour, lemon zest and juice, and superfine sugar. Mix well.

In a separate bowl, whisk the egg whites until they are stiff and fold them into the ricotta mixture.

Place a saucepan over low heat and melt the butter. Once the butter has melted, take the pan off the heat and stir in the crushed crackers.

Spoon the cracker mixture into a 10in springform pan and press it down using the back of the spoon to create the base.

Pour the lemon ricotta mixture over the base. Bake in the oven for 55 minutes.

cook's tip

tempting alternatives

Once you have poured the lemon ricotta mixture into the baking pan, cover with fresh blueberries, raspberries, or white chocolate morsels.

raspberry and rose-water roulade

I love flavoring meringues. You might like to try using orange-blossom or lavender water instead of the rose water. It can even just be added to whipped cream for serving with cakes.

serves 6

For the meringue
5 egg whites
2 teaspoons rose water
1 teaspoon white wine vinegar
1 teaspoon cornstarch, sifted
1 cup superfine sugar

For the filling
1 cup heavy cream
2 teaspoons rose water
1 tablespoon superfine sugar
2¼ cups fresh raspberries

To decorate
fresh raspberries
confectioners' sugar, for dusting

Preheat the oven to 275°F.

To make the roulade, put the egg whites in a clean bowl and whisk with an electric hand whisk until soft peaks form. Fold in the rose water, vinegar, and cornstarch.

Pour in the sugar bit by bit, continuing whisking until stiff peaks form.

Smooth the meringue into a jelly-roll pan, lined with foil, or smooth out into a circular shape to create a round pavlova. Bake in the oven for about 80–90 minutes until golden brown on the outside.

Turn off the oven, leaving the door slightly ajar, and let the meringue cool completely in the oven.

For the filling, lightly beat the cream and then beat in the rose water and superfine sugar.

Spread the rose-water cream evenly over the meringue and sprinkle the raspberries on top. Pull up the foil closest to you and roll the roulade away from you, starting with a short end.

Gently transfer the roulade to a serving dish using a cake slice. Spoon the remaining rose-water cream along the top, decorate with raspberries, and lightly dust with confectioners' sugar.

summer ice cream cake

This is a summer heavenly delight! If you wish, you can add chopped hazelnuts, almonds, or grated chocolate to the mixture and you might also like to try raspberries or blueberries instead of the strawberries.

serves 4

¾ cup + 2 tablespoons heavy cream
6 large meringue shells
1¾ cups strawberries
2 teaspoons sugar

Whip the cream in a bowl and break up the meringue shells.

In a separate bowl, mash the strawberries and sugar together with a fork.

Fold the mashed strawberries into the whipped cream, followed by the crushed meringues.

Line a 1lb loaf pan with plastic wrap and pour in the strawberry and meringue mixture. Cover with more plastic wrap and put in the freezer for 2–3 hours or until frozen.

Take the cake from the freezer just before serving. Remove the plastic wrap from the top, turn the loaf pan over onto a plate or board, and then remove the rest of the plastic wrap.

Slice the cake and serve.

the ultimate lemon tart!

The most important step when making this lemon tart is to chill the pastry shell so that you get a crisp result. You can make the tart the day before; in fact, I think it tastes better the next day.

serves 6

For the sweet pastry shell
1⅓ cups all-purpose flour
1 tablespoon confectioners' sugar
½ cup (just over 1 stick) chilled butter, diced
1 egg yolk, beaten

For the filling
2 eggs, plus 2 egg yolks
grated zest and juice of 3 lemons
¼ cup superfine sugar
¾ cup heavy cream
confectioners' sugar, for dusting

To make the pastry shell, sift together the flour and confectioners' sugar, and then rub in the butter until the mixture resembles bread crumbs. Stir in just enough egg yolk to bring the pastry together. Wrap the pastry in plastic wrap and put in the refrigerator for 30 minutes to chill.

Once the pastry has chilled, line a 9in tart pan with the pastry and put in the refrigerator to chill for a further 20 minutes. (This will give a lovely crisp finish to the pastry once it is baked.)

Preheat the oven to 375°F.

Remove from the refrigerator, cover the pastry with parchment paper, and fill with pie weights. Bake in the oven for 15 minutes.

While the shell is baking, make the filling by placing the eggs and yolks, lemon zest, lemon juice, and superfine sugar in a large bowl and whisking. Slowly whisk in the cream.

Pour the lemon filling into the cooked tart crust. Reduce the heat of the oven to 350°F and bake the tart for 25–30 minutes or until the filling has set around the edges. The rest of the filling will set as it cools.

Remove the tart from the oven and let cool.

Once cooled, sift some confectioners' sugar over the top of the tart.

variation
Try sprinkling 12 raspberries into the lemon filling and pushing them down with the back of a spoon before putting the tart in the oven.

apple pie sunday

I love serving this pie
warm with a dollop of
cinnamon whipped cream.
Just whip together a
generous ¾ cup of heavy
cream with 2 teaspoons
of ground cinnamon—
this is Sunday Heaven!

serves 6-8

For the pastry
2¼ cups all-purpose flour
1 tablespoon sugar
1 teaspoon salt
2¼ sticks chilled butter, diced
1 egg
1 tablespoon white wine vinegar
2 tablespoons water

For the filling
2¼lb apples (variety suitable for cooking),
   peeled, cored, and diced
¾ cup superfine sugar
1 teaspoon ground cinnamon
1 tablespoon lemon juice
pinch of freshly grated nutmeg
1 teaspoon salt
2 tablespoons all-purpose flour
1 egg, beaten

Firstly make the pastry by sifting the flour, sugar, and salt into a large bowl. Rub the butter into the flour until it resembles bread crumbs.

Mix together the egg and vinegar with the water and then mix into the bread crumbs until the dough comes together. Divide the dough into 2 parts, wrap in plastric wrap, and chill in the refrigerator for an hour.

Preheat the oven to 350°F.

Once the pastry is chilled, roll out the 2 pieces of dough on a lightly floured counter to a thickness of ¼in and line a 9in pie pan with one piece of dough.

Place the chopped apples, sugar, cinnamon, lemon juice, nutmeg, salt, and flour in a bowl and toss well. Pour the filling into the pastry-lined pan and cover with the second sheet of pastry.

Crimp the edges with a fork and cut out a cross or heart shape in the middle. Brush with the beaten egg and bake in the oven for 50 minutes or until the pie is golden and cooked.

the decadent picnic

One of my best days last winter was taking a picnic and a ball down to the beach in Ireland with some friends. The food was great, we got to kick the ball around afterward, and it hardly cost us anything. You can't buy memories like that.

I love picnics, every part of them, including shopping at the market for breads and cheeses and buying little treats such as olives, artichokes, and relishes at the deli. I love that everyone brings a dish along and am always astounded by the all-round scrumminess of friends' contributions. There is such a sense of anticipation as everyone lays out their delicious salads, quiches, and tarts on the picnic rug. Afterwards, I lie back in the hazy sunshine and think, "This is it, this is heaven." But not quite, because just then someone reaches into the cooler tote and brings out the homemade cookies.

Not only are picnics a wonderfully enjoyable way to spend time outdoors, they are also such great value. Imagine how much the equivalent food would cost in a restaurant or how much it would cost to take the children out for a treat? With a picnic, you get the food, the family, the friends, and the great outdoors. Picnics are about quality time. When you look back on your life, these are the days you'll remember.

what to pack

- Rug to sit on (plus some extra rugs to throw over your legs if it gets cold)
- Thermos of hot water (for making tea)
- Cups, plates, glasses, and cutlery
- Milk and sugar (kept in jam jars)
- Knife and board
- Cooler tote
- Napkins
- And a camera to capture the memory!

location

Picnics don't always have to take place on a cliff or a beach. You can take a picnic to a concert in the park, when walking by a lake or river, when visiting a nice wooded area, or even when going to a city park for the afternoon. Choose a combination of picnic treats from the tantalizing recipes in this chapter.

Enjoy your picnic!

fabulous sandwich fillers

Here are a few ideas for delicious sandwich fillers. You might also like to try the other ideas for fillings in The Envied Lunchbox, on pages 36–37.

cheesy apple slaw
Mix grated hard cheese with grated apple, chopped scallions, a squeeze of lemon juice, and a little mayonnaise. Delicious with whole-wheat bread or rolls.

salmon and cream cheese bagels
Cut the smoked salmon into bite-size pieces, mix with diced cucumber, cream cheese, and a squeeze of lemon. Delicious spread over bagels.

creamy smoked mackerel
Skin and flake some smoked mackerel fillets, then mix with a little mayonnaise and Greek yogurt. Spread onto thick whole-wheat bread and top with crisp lettuce leaves.

italian roasted vegetable
Roast 1 sliced zucchini, eggplant, and red bell pepper with some olive oil. Once roasted, mix with a little sour cream, lemon juice, and fresh basil. Delicious on a baguette. You could also add in some feta or soft goat cheese.

old-fashioned egg salad

This is delicious, but I also love mixing in some diced cucumber and tomatoes, and then sandwiching the egg salad between 2 slices of white sourdough bread.

serves 4

8 hard-boiled eggs
2 scallions, finely sliced
1 teaspoon Dijon mustard
4 tablespoons mayonnaise
sea salt and freshly ground black pepper

Dice the 8 hard-boiled eggs and place in a large bowl.

Add the scallions, mustard, and mayonnaise. Season with salt and pepper, and mix well.

variation
You can also add 1 tablespoon of capers or pickles or, alternatively, ⅓ cup of diced, cooked thick-cut bacon to make the egg salad even more delicious.

winter coleslaw

Try adding some finely chopped hazelnuts to this recipe for an extra nutty flavor and crunch. It will last for about 1 week in the refrigerator and it always tastes better the day after it has been made. (Pictured opposite.)

serves 6

6½–8 tablespoons Greek yogurt
1 teaspoon Dijon mustard
finely grated zest of 1 lemon
juice of ½ lemon
small red cabbage, finely sliced
2 carrots, grated
½ celeriac, grated
1 tablespoon chopped celeriac leaves (celery or flat-leaf parsley leaves may also be used)
sea salt and freshly ground black pepper

Put the yogurt, mustard, lemon zest and juice in a small bowl, and mix well.

Place all of the vegetables into a large bowl, pour over the liquid, and mix well.

Season with salt and pepper, give the coleslaw one last toss, and it is ready to be eaten!

spring coleslaw

Making spring coleslaw is so simple, and the difference in taste to the store-bought version is vast, so it is well worth making it homemade!

serves 6

4 tablespoons plain yogurt
4 tablespoons mayonnaise
1 tablespoon lemon juice
½ teaspoon Dijon mustard
½ head of white cabbage, very thinly sliced
2 scallions, very thinly sliced
2 carrots, coarsely grated
sea salt and freshly ground black pepper

Mix together the yogurt, mayonnaise, lemon juice, and mustard.

Put all the vegetables into a large bowl and pour over the dressing. Season and mix very well.

The coleslaw will keep for 3 days in a refrigerator.

café de flore's quiche lorraine

Café de Flore is one of my favorite cafés in Paris and the quiche is one of my favorite dishes on the menu. Sunday brunch is always the best time to go there. This is my variation of their famous quiche.

serves 6–8

For the pastry
scant 1¼ cups all-purpose flour, plus extra for dusting
pinch of salt
¾ stick chilled butter, diced, plus extra for greasing
1 egg

For the filling
1⅓ cups grated Cheddar cheese
scant 1 cup diced smoked thick-cut bacon
5 eggs, beaten
½ cup + 2 tablespoons milk
¾ cup + 2 tablespoons half and half
sea salt and freshly ground black pepper
4 tomatoes, sliced (optional)
2 sprigs of fresh thyme

To make the pastry, sift the flour and salt into a large bowl. Rub in the butter until you have a soft bread crumb texture. Add the whisked egg to bring the crumb mixture together to form a firm dough (if needed you can add a little cold water too). Wrap the pastry in plastic wrap and let rest in the refrigerator for 30 minutes.

Roll out the pastry on a lightly floured counter and line a well-buttered 8½in tart dish. Don't cut off the edges of the pastry yet. Chill again.

Preheat the oven to 375°F.

Remove the pie shell from the refrigerator, line the base with parchment paper and then fill with pie weights. Place on a baking sheet and bake blind for 20 minutes. Remove the pie weights and parchment, and return the pie shell to the oven for a further 5 minutes. Reduce the temperature of the oven to 325°F.

Sprinkle the grated cheese over the pie shell.

Fry the bacon pieces until they are crisp then sprinkle them over the top of the cheese.

Combine the eggs with the milk and half and half in a bowl, and season well. Pour the mixture over the bacon and cheese. Add the sliced tomatoes (if using), sprinkle the thyme over the top, and trim the edges of the pastry.

Bake for 30–40 minutes or until set. Remove from the oven and let cool and set further.

Serve in wedges.

pesto ricotta tart

I learned this recipe in Italy. Buy some ready-to-roll phyllo dough, and this recipe will be a cinch to make! It's a fabulous dish to serve when going for a picnic, but also great for lunch or as an appetizer served with a green salad.

serves 4

scant ½ cup (just over ¾ stick) butter, plus extra for greasing
1 large leek, trimmed and thinly sliced
2 large eggs
4 tablespoons light cream
½ cup ricotta
1 cup freshly grated Parmesan cheese
3 tablespoons chunky basil pesto (see page 208 for my Summer Basil Pesto recipe)
2 tablespoons finely chopped fresh parsley leaves
sea salt and freshly ground black pepper
8 sheets of phyllo dough

Preheat the oven to 350°F.

Lightly butter a 9in pie plate and set aside. Heat 1 tablespoon of the butter in a skillet over medium heat. Add the leek and cook, stirring often, until soft. Transfer the leek to a large bowl and let cool.

Whisk the eggs in a medium-size bowl. Add to the leeks along with the ricotta, Parmesan cheese, pesto, parsley, and salt and pepper. Stir to combine and set aside.

Melt the remaining butter. Lay one sheet of phyllo in the prepared pie plate. Brush the phyllo with the melted butter, leaving the outer 1½in rim unbrushed. Repeat with 7 more sheets of phyllo.

Trim the edges to match the shape of the pie plate and pour in the filling. Brush the top of the phyllo rim with butter, and bake in the oven for about 40 minutes or until the edges are golden brown and the filling has set. Cool before serving.

summer savory tart

In the fall, I substitute the tomatoes and zucchini for diced roasted butternut squash or smoked thick-cut bacon for a seasonal change.

serves 6-8

9oz ready-made pie crust
1 tablespoon olive oil
2 zucchini, sliced
10oz cooked new potatoes, sliced
2¼ cups tomatoes, sliced
sea salt and freshly ground black pepper
1 cup grated Gruyère
handful of basil leaves
3 eggs
¾ cup + 2 tablespoons crème fraîche
⅝ cup milk
½ cup freshly grated Parmesan cheese

Preheat the oven to 400°F.

Roll out the pastry to a 12in round and line a deepish, loose-based 8–9in tart pan. Line the pie crust with parchment paper and fill with pie weights. Bake in the oven for 15 minutes, then remove the paper and pie weights and bake for a further 5 minutes until the pie crust is pale golden. Reduce the temperature to 350°F.

Place a skillet or grill pan over medium heat, add the olive oil and fry the zucchini until they are lightly browned on each side.

Layer half the potatoes, zucchini, and tomatoes in the pie crust, season between layers, and sprinkle with a little Gruyère and a few basil leaves. Repeat, finishing with a layer of tomatoes.

Beat together the eggs, crème fraîche, and milk. Season, then stir in the remaining Gruyère and two-thirds of the Parmesan cheese.

Pour this mixture over the filling and sprinkle with the rest of the Parmesan cheese.

Bake in the oven for 35–45 minutes until golden and firm to the touch. Scatter with the remaining basil leaves. Let cool for 10 minutes or so before serving.

lemon and arugula salad

This is delicious served with my Café de Flore's Quiche Lorraine on page 106.

serves 4

generous ¾ cup crème fraîche
grated zest and juice of 1 lemon
1 tablespoon Dijon mustard
1lb 10oz new potatoes, cooked
sea salt and freshly ground black pepper
bunch of fresh arugula

Mix together the crème fraîche, lemon juice and zest, and mustard in a bowl.

Slice the potatoes in half. While they are still warm, mix in the dressing. Season with salt and pepper. Fold in the fresh arugula. Stir gently and let cool.

easy italian pasta salad

Try substituting the mozzarella with a fresh goat cheese or ricotta. You can also serve this hearty pasta salad warm.

serves 4

14oz dried fusilli pasta
1 red bell pepper, seeded
8 cherry tomatoes, halved
12 black olives, halved
7oz mozzarella cheese, cut into
  bite-size pieces
bunch of fresh basil leaves, torn
extra virgin olive oil, for drizzling
sea salt and freshly ground
  black pepper

Preheat the oven to 350°F.

Bring a large saucepan of salted water to a boil and cook the fusilli until it is al dente. Drain the pasta and run it under cold water.

Roast the red bell pepper for 20 minutes.

Transfer the roasted bell pepper to a bowl, cover with plastic wrap, and leave for 10 minutes as this allows the steam to loosen the skin of the pepper.

Remove from the bowl, peel off the skin, and dice the flesh.

Transfer the pasta to a large bowl and mix in the roasted bell pepper, tomatoes, olives, mozzarella, and basil.

Drizzle generously with extra virgin olive oil and season with salt and pepper.

spanish tortilla

I love adding sliced chorizo or red bell peppers to this tortilla. It's also absolutely delicious served with a drizzle of fresh homemade Summer Basil Pesto on top (see page 208).

serves 8

10 free range or organic eggs
2 tablespoons olive oil
3 onions, thinly sliced
1¼lb potatoes, peeled and diced
sea salt and freshly ground black pepper

In a bowl, lightly whisk the eggs. Place an 8in skillet over medium heat and pour in half the olive oil. When the oil is hot, add the onions and potatoes, then reduce the heat and let them cook for 15 minutes, making sure that you come back to the pan every few minutes to stir.

Once the potatoes and onions are cooked, put them in the bowl of whisked eggs, season with salt and pepper, and mix together.

Place the skillet back over a low heat, add the remaining olive oil, and pour in the egg, potato, and onion mixture. Let cook for about 15 minutes or until the egg mixture has set.

Flipping the tortilla over can be a bit tricky, so bear with me! Place a plate over the pan and flip the pan over so that the tortilla comes out onto the plate, cooked side up. Slide the tortilla back into the pan with the cooked side facing upward. Let cook for a further 5 minutes.

Once cooked, you can eat the tortilla either hot or cold. Delicious with a big green salad.

my farmers' market pâté

Years ago I had stalls at various farmers' markets in southern Ireland. This pâté was my best-seller and it still is today in my Canal Café! It will keep for 1 week in a refrigerator.

serves 10

For the pâté
4 sticks butter, softened
1¼lb chicken livers, cleaned
2 tablespoons brandy
1 garlic clove, crushed
2 teaspoons fresh thyme

For the caramelized onions
¼ stick butter
2 onions, sliced
1 tablespoon brown mustard seeds

Melt a pat of the butter in a skillet and add the chicken livers. Cook over medium heat for about 15 minutes, stirring occasionally. When the chicken livers are cooked, there should be no trace of redness in the meat. Transfer the cooked livers to a food processor.

Add the brandy, garlic, and thyme to the skillet and deglaze by scraping up all the tiny pieces of meat and juices from the livers using a whisk—the bottom of the pan is where the real flavor is! Add the brandy mixture to the food processor and blend with the livers. Let cool.

While the livers are cooling, make the caramelized onions. Melt the butter in a saucepan and stir in the onions. Reduce the heat, cover the pan, and let cook for about 5 minutes.

Remove the lid, turn up the heat, and stir in the mustard seeds. Continue cooking until the onions have softened and become a rich brown color. Let cool.

Slowly add the remaining butter to the cooled chicken liver mixture and mix until all the butter has blended. Fold in the caramelized onions.

Transfer the mixture to a large dish, cover, and leave to set in the refrigerator for at least 3 hours.

If you want to preserve the pâté for longer, pour some clarified butter on top before setting in the refrigerator. This way it will keep for up to 2 weeks.

This pâté is delicious served with some hot crunchy white bread.

variation
To make Smoked Bacon and Rosemary Pâté, omit the caramelized onions, thyme, and mustard seeds, and add ½ cup of diced smoked thick-cut bacon when cooking the livers. Replace the thyme with fresh rosemary.

chocolate and almond cake

Now who doesn't love chocolate cake...? This mouthwatering chocolate cake is as intense as it is delicious. I always use Valrhona chocolate when I am making it.

serves 10

5½oz good-quality dark chocolate (minimum 70% cocoa solids), broken into pieces
1⅛ sticks butter
4 eggs, separated
scant ¼ cup superfine sugar
⅝ cup self-rising flour
1 cup ground almonds
slivered almonds for the topping

For the chocolate frosting
5½oz good-quality dark chocolate (minimum 70% cocoa solids), broken into pieces
1⅛ sticks unsalted butter, diced

Preheat the oven to 350°F.

Place the chocolate and butter in a heatproof bowl over a saucepan of gently simmering water. Leave until melted and smooth, stirring every few minutes. Let cool.

Put the egg yolks and superfine sugar in a separate bowl and whisk until thick and creamy. Fold in the cooled chocolate mixture, followed by the flour and then the ground almonds. Mix well.

In another bowl, whisk the egg whites until they form soft peaks. Gently fold into the chocolate mixture until completely combined.

Pour the mixture into a lined 10in springform cake pan and bake in the oven for 45–50 minutes or until just firm to the touch. Remove from the oven and let cool in the pan.

To make the chocolate frosting, place the chocolate in a heatproof bowl over a saucepan of simmering water and whisk in the butter until it has melted. Remove the bowl from the heat and whisk every few minutes while the frosting is cooling.

Once the cake and frosting have cooled, frost the cake with the chocolate frosting, and sprinkle some slivered almonds on top to decorate.

homemade jammie dodgers

I loved Jammie Dodgers as a
child and I guess this is really
my more adult version of the
well-loved British cookie!

makes 12-16

2¼ sticks unsalted butter, softened
2¾ cups all-purpose flour
1 cup confectioners' sugar,
  plus extra for sprinkling
pinch of sea salt
⅔ cup strawberry or raspberry jam

Preheat the oven to 350°F.

Beat the butter until it is light and fluffy. Add the
flour, confectioners' sugar, and salt. Combine
all the ingredients until you have a nice dough.
Wrap the dough ball in plastic wrap and chill in
the refrigerator for 1 hour.

After chilling, roll out the dough and cut into
rounds with a circular-shaped cookie cutter.
Place half of the cookies on a baking sheet
lined with parchment paper.

For the other half of the cookies, cut out a heart
shape in the middle and place on a second
lined baking sheet.

Bake both sets of cookies in the oven for
6–8 minutes. Let cool.

Spread half of the cookies with jam and cover
with the cutout heart cookies.

Sprinkle confectioners' sugar on top.

homemade lemon and lime cordial

Make a big batch of the cordial because it will last for approximately 3 months in a sterilized bottle and it's always so handy to have in the refrigerator.

makes 4 cups

1 tablespoon grated lemon rind
2 teaspoons grated lime rind
¾ cup + 2 tablespoons lemon juice
¾ cup + 2 tablespoons lime juice
1¼ cups superfine sugar
2½ cups boiling water

Place the lemon and lime rind, lemon and lime juice, and superfine sugar in a saucepan. Add the boiling water and stir until the sugar has dissolved. Let cool.

Pour the cordial into a sterilized bottle.

To serve, use one-third of a cup of cordial to two-thirds of a cup of chilled sparkling mineral water or iced water. Serve with thinly sliced lemon and lime and a sprig of mint.

the heavenly afternoon tea

I'm a huge fan of afternoon tea—and I don't mean a tea bag in a mug with a cookie. I'm talking about five different kinds of beautiful little sandwiches, a tea bread with melted butter, fresh buttermilk scones, and wonderful homemade cakes.

Afternoon tea needn't be something traditional and expensive in a grand hotel. You can pull it off with great aplomb at home for very little cost. It's also a wonderful excuse to dust off that china you've been saving and get out your prettiest cloths and napkins. If you don't have a set of china, treat yourself—you can buy sets of beautiful china cheaply in charity thrift stores. The tea has to be perfectly brewed using loose tea and served in china cups and saucers. Trust me, tea really does taste better out of a china cup and it looks so much prettier.

Inviting friends round for afternoon tea is a relaxed and fun thing to do; it also feels a little bit decadent. I enjoy the preparation, too; baking is such a pleasurable way to spend a few hours and I feel so proud when I see my sumptuous cakes and tea breads cooling on the racks. Serving afternoon tea for a friend's birthday or pre-wedding bash can also be a really relaxed alternative to a more formal occasion. You can add a touch of glamor with delicate little cupcakes and delicious macaroons or try my Semolina Cake with Honey and Pistachio. Afternoon tea is a pretty, sweet, buttery affair, but if your friends are anything like mine, they'll love it.

how to make the perfect pot of tea

Fill the teapot with water from the hot faucet to warm it prior to adding tea leaves and boiling water.

Fill the kettle with fresh, cold water.

Just before the kettle begins to boil, pour the warm water from the teapot and add one teaspoon of tea leaves per cup, plus an additional teaspoon "for the pot."

Remove the kettle from the heat right after it comes to a boil, and pour 1 cup per person into the teapot.

Let the tea steep for 3–7 minutes, depending on desired strength.

Add cold whole milk or lemon to the tea cups, according to the preference of your guests.

Pour the tea into the cups, using a tea strainer to catch loose leaves.

finger sandwiches

There is something so decadent about de-crusted finger sandwiches. An afternoon tea is just not right without them! Here are a couple of recipes for egg salad and cucumber and smoked salmon finger sandwiches. Home-cooked ham with mustard and Cheddar cheese is another classic. Both recipes below make 8 finger sandwiches.

egg salad

This is a really comforting filling for an afternoon-tea sandwich.

3 eggs
1 tablespoon crème fraîche
2 teaspoons finely chopped fresh flat-leaf parsley
sea salt and freshly ground black pepper
4 slices of good-quality sliced white bread

Boil the eggs for 8 minutes. Drain and let cool.

Peel the eggs and mash them with the crème fraîche and parsley, and season with salt and pepper. Mix well.

Spread the egg salad on 2 slices of bread and put the remaining slices of bread on top. Cut off the crusts and slice each sandwich into 4 finger sandwiches, making 8 finger sandwiches in total.

cucumber and smoked salmon

A classic combination, this sandwich filling always feels slightly decadent. Be sure to use the best-quality smoked salmon you can find.

1 tablespoon mayonnaise
2 teaspoons fresh dill
4 slices of oak-smoked salmon
10 thin slices of cucumber
sea salt and freshly ground black pepper
4 slices of good-quality sliced whole-wheat bread

Put the mayonnaise and dill in a bowl, and mix well.

Spread the dill mayonnaise on 2 slices of bread and put the salmon slices and cucumber on top. Season to taste.

Place the remaining slices of bread on top. Cut off the crusts and slice each sandwich into 4 finger sandwiches, making 8 finger sandwiches in total.

short scones

These short scones are half way between a plain scone and a shortbread cookie. They taste divine served with clotted cream and homemade jam (see my recipe for Summer Fruit Jam on page 20).

makes 8

2¼ cups all-purpose flour, plus extra for dusting
¼ cup superfine sugar
1 tablespoon baking powder
1 stick butter
1 egg, beaten (plus a little extra for brushing)
½ cup + 2 tablespoons half and half

Sift the flour, sugar, and baking powder into a large bowl.

Grate the butter into the flour and mix together until the mixture resembles bread crumbs.

In a separate bowl, beat together the egg and half and half. Pour into the flour mixture, and bring the liquid and flour together until they form a dough.

Dust both hands with flour and transfer the dough from the bowl to a floured countertop. Roll out the dough until it is about ¾in thick and cut out 8 rounds with a cookie cutter.

Brush lightly with some beaten egg and put in a refrigerator for 1 hour to chill.

Preheat the oven to 425°F.

Bake in the oven for 10 minutes or until the scones are lightly golden brown.

madeleines

Madeleines are deliciously light and so simple to make. The only tricky thing is that you do need a madeleine pan to make these, as it gives the cakes their distinctive shape.

makes 24

1¾ cups all-purpose flour, plus extra for dusting
1 teaspoon baking powder
⅔ cup superfine sugar
4 eggs
1¾ sticks unsalted butter, softened, plus a little extra for greasing
2 teaspoons vanilla extract
2 tablespoons confectioners' sugar

Preheat the oven to 350°F.

Sift the flour and baking powder into a large bowl.

In a separate bowl, whisk together the sugar and eggs with an electric hand whisk until they are fluffy, followed by the butter.

Using a spatula, fold in the flour mixture and vanilla extract. Cover the bowl and put in the refrigerator for 20 minutes to chill.

Grease a 24-hole madeleine pan with butter and dust with flour. Using a spoon, fill each mold with the batter.

Bake in the oven for 10 minutes or until golden in color.

Let cool in the pan for 5 minutes and then tip onto a cooling rack.

Dust with the confectioners' sugar.

semolina cake with honey and pistachio

Yes, it tastes as good as it looks! Sweet, sticky, and with a little crunch, it is one of the most heavenly cakes that I have made.

makes 1 cake

4 large eggs
¾ cup superfine sugar
¼ cup vegetable oil
generous ¾ cup all-purpose flour
¾ cup semolina
1½ teaspoons baking powder
pinch of salt
1½ cups pistachios, finely ground
1 teaspoon grated lemon zest
2 tablespoons pistachios, chopped

For the syrup
generous ¾ cup honey
1 cup water
1 tablespoon lemon juice

Preheat the oven to 350°F.

Place the eggs and sugar in a large bowl, and beat together with a electric hand mixer on high speed for about 5 minutes. Reduce the speed and slowly pour in the vegetable oil.

Add the flour, semolina, baking powder, and salt, and mix well until the batter comes together.

Fold in the ground pistachios and lemon zest.

Pour the cake batter into a greased 10in springform pan and bake in the oven for 30–35 minutes.

Meanwhile, make the syrup by stirring the honey, water, and lemon juice in a saucepan and placing over high heat. Leave the syrup to boil and reduce by half, which takes about 10 minutes.

Use a skewer to poke deep holes in the cake while it is still hot. Drizzle half of the syrup evenly over the top, allowing it to be absorbed, then pour over the remaining syrup. Let cool completely, then sprinkle with the chopped pistachios.

Serve with a spoonful of mascarpone cream.

old-fashioned victoria sponge

Every Saturday when I was a child we would have a Victoria sponge cake (named after Queen Victoria). It's such a simple recipe—just a light sponge with strawberries and cream—but sometimes the simplest things are the best. When fresh strawberries aren't in season, use strawberry jam instead.

makes 1 cake

2 sticks butter, plus extra for greasing
1 cup superfine sugar
4 eggs
1¾ cups self-rising flour
pinch of salt
2 tablespoons warm water
¾ cup + 2 tablespoons whipped cream
2 cups strawberries, hulled and sliced
confectioners' sugar, for dusting

Preheat the oven to 375°F.

Grease and line with parchment paper three 7in cake pans.

In a large bowl, cream together the butter and sugar using a wooden spoon or an electric hand mixer. Beat in the eggs one at a time.

Sift the flour and salt into the bowl, add the warm water, and mix well.

Transfer to the prepared pans and bake in the oven for 15–20 minutes. Let cool.

Place one of the sponges on a cake stand and spread over half of the whipped cream followed by half of the sliced strawberries. Place another sponge on top and repeat, finishing with the third sponge on the top.

Dust with confectioners' sugar.

irish tea brack

This traditional Irish tea brack is a great way of using up all those dried fruits that get leftover after the Christmas baking. The brack will last for up to 2 weeks.

makes 1 loaf

2½ cups mixed dried fruit (raisins, golden raisins, and currants)
1¼ cups cold tea
½ cup superfine sugar
1 egg, beaten
2 cups all-purpose flour
2 teaspoons baking powder
2 teaspoons pumpkin pie spice

Place the dried fruit in a bowl and cover with the cold tea. Leave to soak overnight.

Next day, place the sugar and egg in a bowl. Sift in the flour, baking powder, and pumpkin pie spice and mix all the ingredients together.

Preheat the oven to 350°F.

Pour the soaked fruits and any remaining tea into the bowl and mix together well.

Pour into a greased 2¼lb loaf pan and bake in the oven for 1 hour.

Let cool on a wire rack.

vanilla cupcakes

The vanilla frosting for these dainty little cupcakes can be prepared in advance and stored in an airtight container for up to 3 days.

makes 48 cupcakes

2 sticks butter, softened
1 cup superfine sugar
4 large eggs (at room temperature)
2 cups all-purpose flour
2 teaspoons baking powder
scant 1 cup milk
1 teaspoon vanilla extract

For the vanilla frosting
2 sticks butter, softened
4¾ cups confectioners' sugar
scant ½ cup milk
2 teaspoons vanilla extract

Preheat the oven to 350°F.

In a large bowl, cream the butter until smooth using an electric hand mixer. Add the sugar gradually and beat until the batter is fluffy. Add the eggs, one at a time.

Sift the flour and baking powder into the batter and mix well, gradually adding the milk and vanilla extract.

Using a spatula, scrape around the sides of the bowl and make sure the mixture is thoroughly combined.

Line two 24-cup muffin pans with paper liners and carefully spoon the batter into the cases, filling each one about three-quarters full. Bake in the oven for 20–25 minutes.

Cool the cupcakes in the pans for 15 minutes. Remove from the pans and cool completely on a wire rack.

To make the frosting, put the butter in a large mixing bowl. Add 3¼ cups of the confectioners' sugar, followed by the milk, and vanilla extract. Using an electric hand mixer set at medium speed, beat together until smooth and creamy.

Gradually add the remaining sugar, beating well after each addition, until the frosting is of a good spreading consistency. You may not need to add all of the sugar.

Frost the cooled cupcakes, making sure that the frosting is used at room temperature, as it will set if chilled.

coffee cake

This is a deliciously
light sponge cake with a
heavenly creamy frosting...

makes 1 cake

1¾ sticks butter, softened, plus extra for greasing
scant 1 cup superfine sugar
3 large eggs
1⅔ cups self-rising flour
1 teaspoon baking powder
½ cup finely chopped walnuts
1 tablespoon good espresso coffee
8 walnuts, halved, for decorating

For the frosting
1¼ cup mascarpone
¾ cup confectioners' sugar
2 teaspoons espresso coffee

Preheat the oven to 350°F.

Grease and line with parchment paper two 8in spring-form pans.

Place the butter and sugar in a large bowl and cream together using an electric hand whisk until pale and fluffy. Beat in the eggs one by one.

Sift the flour and baking powder into the bowl and mix well with a wooden spoon. Stir in the chopped walnuts and coffee.

Transfer the cake batter to the two prepared pans. Bake in the oven for 25 minutes or until golden in color. Insert a skewer into the middle of the cakes; if it comes out clean, then the cake is done.

Meanwhile, make the frosting by beating together the mascarpone, confectioners' sugar, and coffee.

Once the cake has cooked, remove from the oven and let cool.

Once cooled, spread half of the frosting over one of the cakes, place the other cake on top, and spread the remainder of the frosting over the top.

Decorate the cake with the halved walnuts.

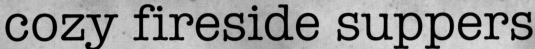

cozy fireside suppers

It's cold outside, I've been chasing my tail all day and my brain is frazzled by a thousand and one phone calls. I just want to curl up in front of the fire with a good bottle of red, old friends, and delicious, undemanding food that I can make in minutes.

When I was a child, we used to call it "Tea on the Knee." It was a huge treat to drop the formality of eating round the table and have our food in front of the television. Even the dog got to sneak up on to the sofa. Cozy fireside suppers aren't out to impress; this is relaxed, unfussy eating with family and friends, serving food that I can make ahead of time and heat through in a few minutes. Every family has its favorites, but in most households, comfort foods, such as Spiced Italian Meatballs and Spaghetti or Creamy Macaroni with Smoked Bacon, go down well.

This is not the time to start worrying about calories—cozy fireside suppers are indulgent, and dessert is a must. Once in a while desserts like Apple and Blackberry Crisp with Vanilla Custard or Orange Rice Pudding with Winter Fruits really don't hurt, far from it. The main thing about this type of meal is that it is non-stress food. It's not going to make any demands on you. You can prepare it in minutes, then grab a glass of wine, bunk up on the sofa with family and friends, and watch your favorite DVD.

spiced italian meatballs and spaghetti

I used to make this dish when I lived in Turin in the north of Italy. The winters would get very cold and, after being out in the snow, this supper dish was so warming and comforting to come home to.

serves 4

9oz ground beef
1 small red chile, finely chopped
2 garlic cloves, crushed
1 egg yolk
sea salt and freshly ground black pepper
¾ cup all-purpose flour
scant ¼ cup olive oil
1 onion, finely chopped
1¼lb canned chopped tomatoes
small bunch of fresh basil leaves, torn
1¼lb spaghetti
1 cup freshly grated Parmesan cheese, to serve

Place the ground beef, chile, garlic, and egg yolk in a large bowl, season with salt and pepper, and mix well.

Roll 2 teaspoons of the meat mixture into a ball, lightly dust in the flour, and set to one side. Repeat with the rest of the meat mixture and place the meatballs in the refrigerator for 30 minutes (this stops them from losing their shape). Note that the meatballs can be prepared the night before.

Place a skillet over medium heat and add the olive oil. Gently sauté the onion in the olive oil until soft.

Add the meatballs and gently fry until golden brown. Add the tomatoes and torn fresh basil leaves. Season to taste, then reduce the heat and let simmer for 10–15 minutes.

Meanwhile, cook the spaghetti in salted boiling water. Drain and add to the sauce. Mix well and serve with freshly grated Parmesan cheese.

cook's tip

quick garlic bread

For some quick garlic bread to serve with the meatballs, crush 4 cloves of garlic and beat in a bowl with 1¾ sticks softened butter. Spread on a sliced ciabatta loaf and place in a preheated oven at 350°F for 15 minutes.

creamy macaroni with smoked bacon

I cook this when I am tired and want something that is comforting, tasty, and quick to cook. Using spicy sausage or smoked tuna instead of the smoked bacon is also delicious!

serves 6

18oz macaroni
1 tablespoon olive oil
¼ cup diced smoked thick-cut bacon
7oz stale white bread
¾ stick butter

For the cheese sauce
⅜ stick butter
½ cup all-purpose flour
2⅜ cups milk
1¾ cups freshly grated Cheddar cheese
¾ cup freshly grated Parmesan cheese
sea salt and freshly ground
    black pepper
1 teaspoon Dijon mustard

Preheat the oven to 350°F.

To make the cheese sauce, melt the butter in a heavy-bottomed saucepan, stir in the flour, and cook for 2 minutes until it resembles a small piece of dough. Slowly whisk in the milk, stirring all the time. Stir in the Cheddar and Parmesan cheese. Season with salt and pepper, add the Dijon mustard, and stir.

Turn down the heat and cook until the sauce starts to thicken (it should coat the back of a wooden spoon). The cheese sauce should be creamy in texture; if it becomes too thick, add more milk.

While the cheese sauce is simmering, add the pasta to a large saucepan of salted boiling water and stir for about 30 seconds so that the pasta doesn't stick together. Cook for about 10 minutes, then drain.

Place a skillet over high heat and add the olive oil. Add the bacon and cook for about 5 minutes until they are nice and crispy.

Pour the pasta into a 10in baking dish, followed by the cooked bacon. Make sure that the bacon is evenly dispersed throughout the pasta. Pour the cheese sauce over the pasta.

Grate the bread (I prefer to do this rather then blitz it in a food processor as it gives a better texture). Place the skillet back over the heat and add the butter. Once the butter has melted, stir in the bread crumbs and cook for 2–3 minutes.

Sprinkle the bread crumbs over the cheesy macaroni and bake in the oven for 40 minutes or until the top is lovely and golden.

authentic lasagna

There are many recipes for lasagna throughout the world, but this one is the most authentic. I learned how to make it when I lived in Italy, and even my Italian friends agreed that it was just how their grandmothers used to make it!

serves 6

2–3 tablespoons olive oil
¼ stick butter, plus a little
   extra for greasing
2 onions, finely diced
1 carrot, finely diced
½ celery stalk, finely diced
2 garlic cloves, crushed
2¼lb freshly ground beef
sea salt and freshly ground
   black pepper
1¾ cups red wine
1¼lb canned chopped tomatoes
bunch of fresh basil leaves, torn
1 cup freshly grated Parmesan cheese
12 fresh lasagna noodles

For the béchamel sauce
¾ stick butter
¾ cup all-purpose flour
3½ cups milk
pinch of freshly grated nutmeg

Place a flameproof Dutch oven over medium heat and add the olive oil and butter, followed by the onions, carrot, celery, and garlic. Stir and cook for 5 minutes until softened.

Stir in the beef and season with salt and pepper. Cook, stirring occasionally, until the beef has turned a light brown color. Pour in the red wine and simmer for about 20 minutes.

Stir in the tomatoes and fresh basil. Lower the heat and let simmer for 1 hour, or more if you can. The longer you allow it to simmer, the more tender the meat becomes.

To make the béchamel sauce, melt the butter in a saucepan, stir in the flour, and cook for 2 minutes until it resembles a small piece of dough. Slowly whisk in the milk, stirring all the time. Turn down the heat and cook until the sauce starts to thicken (it should coat the back of a wooden spoon). Stir in the nutmeg. The béchamel sauce should be creamy in texture; if it becomes too thick, add more milk.

Preheat the oven to 350°F.

Grease a shallow baking dish. Pour a layer (about ½in deep) of meat sauce into the baking dish so that it covers the base. Follow with a thin layer of béchamel sauce and a grating of Parmesan cheese. Place a layer of lasagna noodles on top. Continue with two or three more layers. Finally, smear a layer of béchamel sauce on top of the last lasagna noodles followed by a final generous sprinkling of Parmesan.

Bake in the oven for about 40 minutes until bubbling all over and a knife slips easily through the layers of lasagna.

risotto with wild mushrooms

I learned how to make a risotto properly when I lived in Italy. It's a simple dish to make, but you need to follow the steps, sautéeing the shallots, toasting the rice, and adding the stock bit by bit. There are so many different exciting combinations—why not try asparagus and ricotta; roasted red bell peppers, basil, and mascarpone; smoked chicken, Parmesan cheese, and tarragon; or butternut squash and sage?

serves 6

scant ½ cup (just over ¾ stick) butter
1 onion, very finely chopped
2 garlic cloves, chopped
1¼ cups risotto rice
½ cup + 2 tablespoons dry white wine
4 cups hot vegetable stock
2 tablespoons olive oil
9oz mixed wild mushrooms
sea salt and freshly ground black pepper
sprig of fresh sage, finely chopped
¾ cup freshly grated Parmesan cheese

Melt ⅔ stick of the butter in a large saucepan, add the onion and half of the garlic, and cook gently for 3–4 minutes until softened.

Add the rice and stir for a minute or so to coat it in the butter. Pour in the white wine and let it bubble for a few minutes to allow the alcohol to evaporate.

Every couple of minutes, add some stock, stir, and allow the rice to absorb the juices. Repeat until all of the stock has been absorbed.

Meanwhile, heat the olive oil in a large skillet over medium heat, add the remainder of the garlic, and cook for a minute.

Follow with the wild mushrooms and cook for a further 2–3 minutes. Season with salt and pepper.

When the rice is tender and all the stock has been absorbed, remove from the heat and let rest for 30 seconds.

Stir in the mushrooms, the remaining butter, the sage, and Parmesan cheese.

Season to taste and serve immediately.

···· cook's tip ····

buying risotto rice

The most common variety of risotto rice that you can buy is arborio, but the best variety is carnaroli and the second-best is baldo.

warming cottage pie

Now, I can't think of anything more fabulous than curling up in front of a real fire on a cold evening with a big bowl of cottage pie in my lap... When I am making cottage pie, I always double the recipe and freeze a dish for those extra-lazy days.

serves 6

2 tablespoons olive oil
1 onion, diced
1 garlic clove, crushed
2 carrots, diced
1¾lb ground beef
4 teaspoons tomato paste
1¼ cups hot beef stock
1½ cups frozen peas
sea salt and freshly ground black pepper
2¼lb creamy mashed potatoes
¾ stick butter, melted

Preheat the oven to 350°F.

Place a flameproof Dutch oven over medium heat and add the olive oil. When the oil is hot, add the onion, garlic, and carrots, then cover, reduce the heat, and cook for 5 minutes.

Remove the lid and turn up the heat to high. Add the ground beef and cook until brown.

Stir in the tomato paste, beef stock, and frozen peas. Season with salt and pepper, and simmer over a low heat for 15 minutes.

Cover the mixture with the mashed potato and brush the top with melted butter to get a crispy golden finish.

Cook in the oven for 50 minutes.

vegetable curry

This vegetable curry is just bursting with flavor. You can add chicken or shrimp to the curry if you wish.

serves 4

18oz potatoes, left whole if small
   and cut in half if big
scant ¼ cup olive oil
2 onions, chopped
4 garlic cloves, crushed
2in piece fresh ginger, peeled
   and crushed
1 teaspoon turmeric powder
2 teaspoons ground cumin seeds
1 eggplant, cut into wedges
18 green beans, cut into wedges
14oz canned chopped tomatoes
2 teaspoons ground coriander
3 tablespoons natural yogurt
sea salt and freshly ground black pepper

cook's tip

curry secrets

• You can add chicken to this curry; if you do, just omit the eggplant.

• If you can get your hands on fresh coriander seeds, then use these instead and stir them in just before serving.

• This curry always tastes better the day after it's made!

Half fill a saucepan with water, add the potatoes and place over high heat. When the water starts to boil, reduce the heat, pour off half the liquid, and simmer until the potatoes are slightly tender. Drain the potatoes, let cool, and cut into wedges.

Put a splash of the olive oil in a saucepan over medium heat and add the potatoes, onions, garlic, ginger, turmeric powder, and cumin seeds. Cook until the potatoes are golden, stirring all the time. Remove to a plate and keep warm.

Pour the remaining olive oil into the pan and leave to heat up before adding the eggplant and green beans. Cook for 5 minutes.

Return the spicy potato mixture to the pan and stir in the tomatoes, ground coriander, and yogurt.

Season with salt and pepper and let simmer over low heat for about 10 minutes.

Serve with basmati rice.

fondue to share

When I lived in Italy, we used to drive up to the Alps on winter Sundays and head to one of the many cabin-style bistros for a warming fondue. They are so delicious and fun to make, eat, and share...

serves 4

1 garlic clove
½ cup dry white wine
7oz Fontina cheese
7oz Reblochon (or Brie, Tomme, or Raclette) cheese
pinch of freshly grated nutmeg
1 tablespoon cornstarch
2 tablespoons kirsch
sea salt and freshly ground black pepper

Rub the interior of a stainless-steel saucepan with the garlic clove, then discard the garlic.

Add the white wine and bring to a simmer over medium heat.

Add the Fontina and Reblochon cheeses and the nutmeg. Cook, stirring with a wooden spoon, until the cheese melts.

Combine the cornstarch with the kirsch in a small bowl. Mix thoroughly and stir into the cheese mixture.

Continue to simmer and stir until the cheese mixture becomes smooth (which should take about 5 minutes), then season with salt and pepper. Add in a splash more white wine if the fondue is too thick.

Transfer to a fondue pot and set over a flame.

Serve with an assortment of pickles, home-cooked ham, and chunks of country-loaf bread, using a fondue fork to dip the pieces of food into the sauce.

moules and frites

This is such a simple dish to prepare and great for feeding large numbers of guests. The only trick is that the mussels need to be cooked at the last minute. For this reason, I would suggest having them all prepared and stored in the refrigerator so that you just need to place them in the pot with the other ingredients about 10 minutes before serving.

serves 2

For the French fries
1 cup vegetable oil
1 potato, sliced into thin chips
sea salt

For the moules marinière
1½ tablespoons butter
1 shallot, diced
1 garlic clove, crushed
⅜ cup white wine
2¼lb mussels, cleaned and beards
   removed (discard any that do not
   close when tapped)
scant ¼ cup heavy cream
sea salt and freshly ground
   black pepper
2 tablespoons chopped fresh parsley

Preheat the oven to 125°F.

Make the French fries by heating the oil in a deep, heavy-bottomed saucepan until it is very hot. Add the fries and fry for 2–3 minutes until they are golden. Remove with a slotted spoon and drain on some paper towels.

Toss the fries in sea salt and place in the oven, just to keep warm while you cook the mussels.

Prepare the mussels by placing the butter in a saucepan over medium heat, stir in the shallot and garlic, and let cook for a minute.

Pour in the white wine and leave for a further 2–3 minutes.

Allow to heat through, and then add the mussels and cook for 4–5 minutes or until all the mussels have opened. Discard any unopened mussels.

Add the cream and continue to cook uncovered for 2–3 minutes.

Season with salt and pepper and sprinkle the chopped parsley on top.

Transfer to a large warmed bowl and serve with the fries.

homemade parmesan gnocchi with creamy gorgonzola sauce

There are so many delicious ways to eat gnocchi. Here are some of my favorites: fresh sage gently fried in butter and wrapped over the gnocchi; spicy tomato sauce and Parmesan cheese; small cubes of roasted butternut squash and ricotta. Does this sound tempting…?

makes 16

For the gnocchi
14oz russet or Idaho potatoes, whole and unpeeled
scant ½ cup all-purpose flour, plus extra for dusting
½ cup freshly grated Parmesan cheese, plus extra for serving
1 egg, beaten
pinch of sea salt and freshly ground black pepper

For the creamy Gorgonzola sauce
2 tablespoons butter
2 tablespoons half and half
2½oz Gorgonzola

To make the gnocchi, cook the potatoes in very little water. Once cooked, peel and mash them well or put through a potato ricer.

Mix in the flour, Parmesan cheese, egg, salt, and pepper, and stir well.

Turn the dough out onto a lightly floured countertop and knead gently until it is well combined. Shape into three or four balls.

Dust the counter with more flour if necessary. Using your fingertips, roll the dough into a sausage, about ¾in in diameter. Cut the dough into 1in pieces and roll the gnocchi against the front of a fork to create ridges. (This will help to hold the sauce on the gnocchi once it is cooked.)

To make the sauce, place a saucepan over low heat and melt the butter, half and half, and Gorgonzola gently for about 3–4 minutes.

Meanwhile, bring a large saucepan of salted water to a boil and add the gnocchi. When they have risen to the surface of the water, they are cooked, so remove quickly and drain.

Add the gnocchi to the saucepan with the creamy Gorgonzola sauce and mix gently.

Transfer to serving plates and sprinkle with the extra grated Parmesan.

cozy fireside suppers

homemade feta and sun-dried tomato sausages

Children love helping to make these sausages. There are lots of variations that you can try, including sage and grated apple; garlic and thyme; or cajun-spiced. I love eating my sausages with wet polenta or creamy whipped potatoes.

serves 5

8 semi sun-dried tomatoes, finely chopped
1lb ground free-range pork
 (from the neck or shoulder)
3oz feta cheese
1 tablespoon dried oregano
1 egg, beaten
sea salt and freshly ground black pepper
all-purpose flour, for dusting
olive oil, for frying

Put the sun-dried tomatoes in a mixing bowl with the ground pork, feta cheese, dried oregano, and beaten egg. Season with salt and pepper, and mix well.

Divide the mixture into 10 pieces and roll each one into a sausage shape.

Sprinkle a thin layer of all-purpose flour on a baking sheet and roll the sausages in the flour. Rock the sausages back and forth in your hands to remove any excess flour. You want the sausages to be very lightly coated in the flour.

Put the sausages on a clean tray and leave to chill in a refrigerator for 1 hour (this will help the sausages to hold their shape).

Place a skillet over medium heat and add some olive oil. Add the sausages one by one and gently cook for about 10 minutes, turning every couple of minutes to make sure that they are evenly cooked.

Serve with creamy mashed potatoes or wet polenta (see Cook's Tip, left).

cook's tip

making wet polenta

Pour 4 cups of water into a large saucepan, add 1 tablespoon of sea salt, and place over high heat. When the water has come to a boil, whisk in 2¼ cups of polenta and turn the heat down to the lowest possible setting. With a wooden spoon, keep stirring the polenta every few minutes—it takes about 10–15 minutes to cook. Then, season with freshly ground black pepper and mix in some olive oil.

orange rice pudding
with raspberry jam

This was my favorite dessert as a child and I still get cravings for it. It's so cheap to make and a great stand-by dessert as well. I love to cook these rice puddings in little individual ceramic pots to serve at a dinner party and put a nice big jar of jam in the center of the table so that everyone can just help themselves.

serves 2

2 tablespoons butter
generous ¼ cup short-grain rice
grated zest and juice of 1 orange
¼ cup superfine sugar
⅓ cup golden raisins
1 teaspoon freshly grated nutmeg
3¾ cups milk
jar of homemade raspberry jam

Preheat the oven to 325°F.

Grease a 2½pt pie dish with 2 teaspoons of the butter.

Put the rice, orange zest, sugar, golden raisins, and nutmeg in a bowl, and mix well. Pour the rice mixture into the prepared pie dish.

Pour the milk and orange juice over the rice. Slice the remaining butter and place on top.

Bake in the oven for 1½ hours, stirring a couple of times.

Serve with the homemade raspberry jam.

variation
You can make a Rose-water Rice Pudding by omitting the orange juice and zest and adding 2 tablespoons of rose water. This is delicious served with fresh raspberries.

apple and blackberry crisp with vanilla custard

Now who doesn't love a warm fruity crisp served with a big spoonful of cream? Try sprinkling 1 tablespoon of extra brown sugar on top just before it goes in the oven, to get an extra crunchy top.

serves 6

For the filling
18oz apples (suitable variety for cooking)
generous ½ cup sugar
1 tablespoon water
1½ cups blackberries

For the crisp
¾ stick chilled butter, diced
1¼ cups all-purpose flour
¼ cup brown sugar
scant ½ cup chopped hazelnuts

For the custard
2¼ cups milk
1 vanilla bean, slit
3 egg yolks
1¾ tablespoons superfine sugar
1 teaspoon cornstarch

Preheat the oven to 400°F.

To make the filling, put the apples, sugar, and water into a saucepan and simmer until the apples are beginning to break down (you don't want to end up with a mush because the apples are going to be cooked further in the oven). Remove from the heat, stir in the blackberries, and let cool.

Meanwhile, make the crisp by rubbing the butter into the flour. Add the sugar and chopped hazelnuts.

Put the filling in an ovenproof pie dish or into individual ramekin dishes, and sprinkle the crisp on top. Bake in the oven for 45 minutes if you are using a pie dish and 25 minutes if you are using individual ramekins, or until the crisp is golden in color.

While the crisp is cooking, make the custard by heating the milk with the vanilla bean over medium heat until it comes to a simmer, then remove from the heat.

Mix together the egg yolks, sugar, and cornstarch until you get a smooth paste.

Place the milk back over the heat and stir in the egg mixture. Reduce the heat to low and continue to stir the custard until it thickens.

Remove the vanilla bean (rinse it under water and dry it so that you can use it again).

---

cook's tip

using old vanilla beans

You can make vanilla sugar by placing used vanilla beans in the center of a large jar of superfine sugar and giving the jar a good shake to make sure the vanilla is buried. Within a week the sugar will be scented with vanilla. Great for baking!

banana bread pudding

I also love making this pudding with brioche and sprinkling chocolate morsels through the layers for a really decadent bread pudding. Delicious served with the Vanilla Custard on the opposite page.

serves 6

¼ stick butter, plus extra for greasing
10 thin slices of bread
2 bananas, sliced
2 teaspoons ground cinnamon
1¼ cups milk
½ cup + 2 tablespoons half and half
2 free range or organic eggs
2 tablespoons brown sugar
pinch of freshly grated nutmeg

Preheat the oven to 375°F.

Grease a 2½pt pie dish with butter.

Spread each slice of bread on one side with butter and cut into triangles.

Arrange a layer of bread, buttered-side up, in the bottom of the dish, then add a layer of banana. Sprinkle with a little cinnamon, then repeat the layers of bread, banana, and cinnamon until you have used up all of the bread. Finish with a layer of bread, and set aside.

Gently warm the milk and half and half in a saucepan over low heat.

Crack the eggs into a bowl, add the sugar, and whisk lightly.

Add the warm milk and cream mixture to the whisked eggs, and stir well.

Pour over the prepared bread layers and push the bread down using a wooden spoon to make sure that it is completely covered in the liquid.

Sprinkle with nutmeg and let stand for 30 minutes.

Bake in the oven for 30–40 minutes or until the custard has set and the top is a golden brown color.

Making a selection of dips yourself will make your guests feel really special.

Homemade Vanilla Fudge, Hot Chocolate Mix, or Cookie Dough are lovely gifts for your guests to take home.

A bowl of warming soup is the perfect appetizer for a dinner party on a cold winter's night.

the divine dinner party

homemade table settings

apéritifs

simple dinner party menus

homemade edible gifts

homemade table settings

When I think about the most memorable meals I've eaten, I also remember the location and the table setting. The table setting gives a first impression and sets the tone, creating a sense of occasion, atmosphere, and mood. I have three golden rules. First, keep it seasonal, following the flowers, fauna, colors, and mood of the time of year; second, bear in mind that you want your guests to enjoy themselves; and third, keep it simple by avoiding conflicting patterns in the tablecloth and napkins and by using the same type or color of flowers. And, for heaven's sake, avoid overhead lights and instead use candles or little lamps to give a soft flattering light. Try to match the accessories to the occasion, whether this is festive, glamorous, romantic, or magical. At Christmas, for example, what could be easier than taking a piece of ribbon and tying a name card to the back of each guest's chair with a sprig of holly and fir? Or, for spring, pick a handful of wild flowers, such as daisies, and tie three on each napkin with a yellow ribbon. It is so simple, yet will really delight your guests. And that's the thing, it's not about expense, but about using what's readily available, as well as personal flair to surprise, inspire, or amuse them.

alfresco dining

this page The most elegant tables are often the simplest. Daisies look so beautiful tied with a piece of ribbon and placed on your guests' napkins. You could also tie a flower to the backs of the chairs. Fresh flowers look wonderful, but a few sprigs of dried lavender also look great.

mid-summer night supper

above and left Seasonal flowers are always the most beautiful and a single flower on each plate makes such a statement. Use old vases, perhaps made from pewter, to give the table a natural look.

below Match the colors of the accessories on the table. Here, the mustard-colored velvet ribbons that I used to tie the napkins work beautifully with the lavender color of the irises.

christmas party

above left and top right
Wrap ivy leaves around a piece of wire to create a natural-looking wreath. Put a candle in a glass night-light holder and hang it from the wreath with ribbon.

above right Make a menu card for each guest. They are simple to make and some red velvet ribbon adds a festive touch.

far left A sprig of pine and laurel, velvet ribbon, and a name card attached to the back of each chair look so pretty.

left Wrap some pretty ribbon around plain candlestick holders.

inexpensive decorating tips

Here are just a few simple, but effective, suggestions for making your dinner-party setting look beautiful:

Type up the menu that you will be serving and print it out on some sea-blue paper. Then, place the menus on peoples' plates with a sea-shell or pine cone holding them down.

Buy a roll of brightly colored ribbon and cut it into 6in strips. Roll up the napkins and tie a bow around each one with the ribbon strips.

Use seasonal vegetables as table centerpieces. A big bowl of lemons or eggplant looks so pretty in the center of a table (and you can use the vegetables afterward too).

In summer, put tea-lights inside jam and Mason jars. They look so pretty and you can place them around the patio or garden—such an inexpensive way of creating a great atmosphere.

In winter, snip off some sprigs of rosemary or thyme in your garden and place them in colorful glasses. Line these up along the center of the table. Not only do they look beautiful, but they smell wonderful too!

apéritifs

Having friends around for a party is such a fun thing to do and it really doesn't have to be stressful at all. I remember the first time I threw a New Year's Eve party, I must have changed the menu at least a thousand times. Now, I just want everyone to enjoy the food and relax.

With a little planning, some helpful tips, and simple recipes, your party will be wonderful. Dips and platters are a fabulous (and super-easy!) way to present food at a party because you can have them all prepared the day before with just the pita chips for dipping to roast before guests arrive. Try making my recipe for Warming Cottage Pie (see page 141) or smaller versions of my Homemade Feta and Sun-dried Tomato Sausages (see page 150) and roasting them in the oven—these are the pinnacle of comfort food and will be sure to warm the hearts of your hungry guests. You can also make individual pies in ramekins, which can be made the night before.

A line of the delicious Lemon Meringue Angels in this chapter served in shot glasses on a tray is so beautiful and the best part is that they can also be prepared the night before and left to wait in the refrigerator for their grand entrance. This leaves you ample time to have a lovely, relaxing bubble bath, enjoying one of the many cocktails you'll find over the next few pages, before slipping into your best number. It is after all your party!

torino mojito!

This is my favorite cocktail to drink in the summer. It's so full of delicious zesty flavors. It is a fantastic cocktail for parties.

makes 1

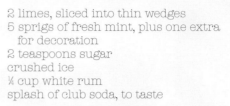

2 limes, sliced into thin wedges
5 sprigs of fresh mint, plus one extra for decoration
2 teaspoons sugar
crushed ice
¼ cup white rum
splash of club soda, to taste

Put the limes (holding back 3 wedges for decoration), mint, and sugar in a sturdy glass and mash so that all the juices in the limes and mint are released.

Add the ice, white rum, and a splash of club soda.

Mix well and decorate with wedges of lime and a sprig of fresh mint.

Every time I visit Paris, I head for the wonderful George V Hotel before or after dinner for their champagne cocktail. So, here's a taste of my favorite cocktail in Paris...!

makes 1

george v champagne cocktail

cook's tip

making sweet salted almonds

Take 1 cup of blanched whole almonds, 1 teaspoon of butter, 1 teaspoon of coarse sea salt, and 2 teaspoons of maple syrup. Place all the ingredients in a large bowl and mix well. Spread the coated almonds on a baking sheet and toast in a preheated oven at 400°F for about 10 minutes or until golden. Let cool.

1 sugar cube
2 dashes of Angostura bitters
generous ½ cup champagne
1 tablespoon cognac
1 orange, quartered

Soak the sugar cube in a champagne flute with the Angostura bitters.

Pour the champagne and cognac over the sugar and bitters.

Garnish with a quarter slice of orange.

pimm's for wimbledon

I adore drinking Pimm's in the summer. Fabulous to drink while watching Wimbledon, on a picnic, or at a summer party.

makes 1 pitcher

1 part Pimm's
1 slice orange
1 slice lemon
2 slices cucumber
1 sliced strawberry
sprig of mint
ice cubes
3 parts lemon soda pop

Pour the Pimm's into a large pitcher, followed by all of the fruit and the fresh mint.

Add the ice cubes and top up with the lemon soda pop. Stir lightly, and serve.

sparkling sicilia

I had this delicious cocktail in Sicilia (Sicily, in southern Italy). Simply multiply the quantities to make a larger batch.

makes 1

generous ⅓ cup Prosecco
1 tablespoon Grand Marnier
⅛ cup fresh orange juice
1 teaspoon superfine sugar

Pour the Prosecco into a champagne flute and mix in the Grand Marnier, fresh orange juice, and sugar. Stir and serve.

sangria

I learned how to make this cocktail when I was a bartender one summer at the White Dog on Nantucket Island. For a plusher version, top it off with some champagne!

makes 1 pitcher

4 oranges
1 unwaxed lemon
1 bottle Pinot Noir or other light red wine
5 tablespoons superfine sugar
ice cubes

Thinly slice 1 orange and the lemon.

Juice the 3 remaining oranges into a pitcher and add the wine and sugar. Stir well, then add the sliced fruit and chill.

Pack in a portable sealed pitcher and serve at the beach in glasses filled with ice.

negroni

While we were shooting this book in France, Francesco (the photographer's assistant) made this cocktail for the whole crew. Everyone loved the cocktail and poor Francesco was on full Negroni-making duties until the early hours!

makes 1

⅛ cup Campari
⅛ cup red Martini
⅛ cup gin
4 ice cubes
slice of orange

Pour the Campari, red Martini, and gin into a cocktail shaker, followed by the ice cubes, and shake well. Leave for 10 minutes to chill.

Serve in a large tumbler with a slice of orange.

i'll take a manhattan!

Nothing beats a real Manhattan!

makes 1

scant ¼ cup bourbon
⅛ cup sweet red vermouth
1 dash Angostura bitters
twist of orange zest, to garnish

Place the bourbon, vermouth, and Angostura bitters into a large glass filled with ice, and stir well.

Strain into a cocktail glass and garnish with the orange twist.

baba ghanoush

This ticks all the boxes—zesty, sweet, creamy, and spicy. It's super-delicious!

serves 4

1 tablespoon olive oil
2 garlic cloves, chopped
½ eggplant, cubed
scant ¼ cup sesame seeds
⅓ cup Greek yogurt
1 bunch of fresh cilantro
juice of 1 lemon
sea salt and freshly ground black pepper

Place a skillet over medium heat and add the olive oil. Add the garlic cloves and eggplant, and fry for 7–8 minutes.

Transfer the garlic and eggplant to a food processor. Add the sesame seeds, Greek yogurt, fresh cilantro, lemon juice, salt and pepper, and blitz to a purée.

Transfer to a bowl and serve.

guacamole

This dip is delicious served with a big bowl of tortilla chips or my Spicy Pita Chips (see page 173).

serves 2

1 ripe avocado
1 garlic clove, crushed
2 tablespoons freshly squeezed lemon or lime juice
1 tablespoon extra virgin olive oil
1 tablespoon chopped fresh cilantro
sea salt and freshly ground black pepper

Cut the avocado in half, remove the pit (keeping it for later), and scoop out the flesh. Mash with a fork, add the garlic, lemon or lime juice, olive oil, and cilantro, and mix well.

Season to taste with the salt and pepper, push the avocado pit into the guacamole and cover with plastic wrap. Doing this will help the guacamole hold its green color.

white bean dip

dukkah

salsa verde

spicy pita chips

Try adding some finely chopped fresh cilantro to the mix because the color looks great, but go easy on the cayenne pepper as it is quite hot.

serves 10

5 tablespoons olive oil
1 garlic clove, crushed
2 teaspoons cayenne pepper
10 pita rounds (each 5in in diameter)
sea salt and freshly ground black pepper

Preheat the oven to 350°F.

Put the olive oil, garlic, and cayenne pepper into a large bowl and whisk together.

Cut the pita rounds into wedges (6 wedges per piece of pita bread) and put in the large bowl with the spicy oil. Stir well, making sure that the pita wedges are thoroughly coated with the oil.

Place the pita breads on a baking sheet and bake in the oven for 15 minutes or until they are slightly crispy.

Serve the pita chips warm or cool with dips.

------ cook's tip ------

marinating olives

Put 1½ cups of mixed green and black olives into a bowl. If the olives are in brine, drain and rinse them first. Toss with a generous amount of olive oil, the grated zest of 1 lemon, 1 teaspoon of dried red chile flakes, 2 sprigs of rosemary (crushed), some sea salt, and 1 garlic clove (thinly sliced). Let marinate, at least overnight.

dukkah dip

This is a delicious, spicy Egyptian dip that is so easy to make and incredibly light.

serves 10

¾ cup sesame seeds
¾ cup blanched almonds
¾ cup coriander seeds
2½ tablespoons cumin seeds
pinch of sea salt and freshly ground
   black pepper
½ cup extra virgin olive oil

Toast all the seeds and almonds together in a hot dry skillet. Keep stirring until fragrant, then let cool.

Once the seeds and almonds have cooled, grind them together with a good pinch of sea salt and freshly ground pepper.

Place the dukkah mix in a bowl and cover with the extra virgin olive oil.

salsa verde

This dip is delicious served with toasted focaccia bread or my Italian Rosemary Crispbreads (see page 88).

serves 4

4 sprigs of fresh basil
1 tablespoon white wine vinegar
sprig of parsley
2 garlic cloves, crushed
2 anchovy fillets, chopped
2 tablespoons capers
½ cup + 2 tablespoons extra virgin olive oil

Tear the basil leaves from the stems and put in a food processor with the rest of the ingredients. Blend for 1 minute.

white bean dip

This dip can be made in minutes and is also great as the recipe is made up of ingredients from the pantry.

serves 10

2 x cans of cannellini beans
   (1lb once drained and rinsed)
2 teaspoons paprika, plus a little
   extra for sprinkling
6 tablespoons extra virgin olive oil
juice of 2 lemons
2 garlic cloves, crushed (optional)
coarse sea salt and freshly
   ground black pepper

In a food processor, combine the cannellini beans, paprika, olive oil, lemon juice, and garlic (if using).

Puree until you reach a smooth consistency.

Season with salt and pepper, and puree again for 20 seconds.

Scoop the white-bean dip into a serving bowl and lightly sprinkle some paprika over the top.

Serve with Spicy Pita Chips (see page 173).

---

cook's tip

making devils-on-horseback

My all-time favorite Christmas party food are Devils-on-Horseback. They are so easy to prepare and extremely rich, tasty, and indulgent. Just soak some prunes in brandy overnight, wrap each one in a piece of bacon, and broil until the bacon is crisp. The sweetness and softness of the prunes works fantastically with the crisp saltiness of the bacon. Probably not the healthiest option, but it is Christmas after all!

pink hummus

You get a fabulous pink color from the beets in this recipe and it makes the dip super healthy! If you don't like beets, just replace them with a generous ⅓ cup of Greek yogurt.

serves 10

2 fresh beets
2 garlic cloves
15oz can of chickpeas, drained
juice of 1 lemon
4 tablespoons olive oil
sea salt and freshly ground
   black pepper

To serve
pita bread
sliced fennel
sliced carrots

Place both whole beets in a saucepan with a little water and bring to a boil. Cover with a lid and let cook for about 25 minutes. You can test to see if the beets are ready by pushing back the skins with your thumb—if the skins come off easily, then the beets are done.

Once the beets are cooked, peel off the skins and chop roughly.

Put the beets, garlic, and chickpeas in a food processer and process until well blended.

Add the lemon juice and olive oil through the feed tube to make a fairly coarse paste. Season with salt and pepper.

Spoon into a serving bowl and serve with the pita, fennel, and carrots.

fresh raita

Delicious served with my Spicy Pita Chips (see page 173).

serves 4

¾ cup + 2 tablespoons Greek yogurt
½ cucumber, diced
1 teaspoon ground cumin
1 tablespoon chopped fresh mint
1 tablespoon chopped fresh cilantro

Mix all of the ingredients together in a bowl.

zaalouk

I make this dip on my Moroccan course at my cooking school and it's one of my favorite dips. It is really delicious served with toasted slices of baguette.

serves 4

2 large eggplant
3 large tomatoes
½ cup + 2 tablespoons olive oil
2–3 garlic cloves, chopped
½ teaspoon sweet paprika
juice of 1 lemon, to taste
  (less may be needed)
1 tablespoon chopped fresh cilantro
sea salt
ground cumin, to dust

Preheat the oven to 350°F.

Put the eggplant on a baking sheet and bake for about 30 minutes until soft when pressed.

Put the tomatoes in an ovenproof dish with half of the oil and roast for about 5–10 minutes.

Remove both the eggplant and tomatoes from the oven and let cool.

Cut the eggplant in half, scoop out the flesh, and chop to a pulp.

Skin the tomatoes, remove the seeds, and chop the flesh to a pulp.

Heat the other half of the oil in a skillet, add the garlic and fry (but don't color). Add the tomatoes, eggplant, and paprika, and fry gently for about 5–10 minutes, stirring regularly to stop the bottom from burning.

Add the lemon juice, cilantro, and salt to taste.

Pour into a bowl and dust with cumin. Eat either warm or at room temperature with some bread.

smoked salmon pâté

This pâté takes all of 5 minutes to make! It's a superb recipe...everyone loves it. You can substitute the smoked salmon for smoked mackerel if you wish.

serves 4

9oz smoked salmon
¼ cup cream cheese
scant ¼ cup crème fraîche
juice of 1 lemon
sea salt and freshly ground black pepper

Place all the ingredients in a food processor and puree until you reach a smooth consistency.

Serve with pita bread, crackers, or crusty bread.

easy florentines

These are divine served as
a sweet canapé or at the end
of dinner with a coffee.

serves 10

3½oz good-quality dark chocolate
  (minimum 70% cocoa solids)
3½oz milk chocolate
3½oz white chocolate
⅛ cup slivered almonds
⅛ cup raisins
1 tablespoon sliced candied cherries
1 tablespoon sliced candied oranges
1 tablespoon sliced candied limes or lemons

Melt the three types of chocolate very slowly in
separate heatproof bowls, each suspended over
a saucepan of simmering water.

Take teaspoons of the melted chocolates and
spread each teaspoon onto sheets of parchment
paper to form even-size disks.

Press one piece of each of the other ingredients
into the melted chocolate, and put in a cool place
to set.

little lemon meringue angels

Sweet, crunchy, and creamy!
These are sweet little angels.

serves 10

6 meringue shells (medium-size)
¾ cup + 2 tablespoons heavy cream
⅔ cup lemon curd (page 22)
grated zest of 1 lemon

Break the meringue shells into small pieces and place in a bowl.

Whip the cream until it forms soft peaks, and fold into the meringue pieces.

Fold the lemon curd into the cream and meringue mixture.

Using a spoon, fill 10 small glasses with the lemon meringue mixture and finish by grating over the lemon zest.

Place in a refrigerator to chill.

------ cook's tip ------

juicing lemons

Try massaging the lemons before juicing to loosen up the skin. This will release up to 50 percent more juice from the lemon. And, don't discard used lemon skins; instead, pop them on the radiator and they will give off a delicate lemon scent as they warm up!

simple dinner party menus

Some of my fondest and most precious memories are of friends and family sharing a homemade meal across the dinner table in my home. Whether it is a celebration or an impromptu gathering, there is nothing better than sharing a cozy supper with the people you love. In fact, dinner parties really have become my favorite pastime!

While the thought of hosting a dinner party might be overwhelming, it really does not have to be. When you use ingredients that are fresh, local, seasonal, and, of course, delicious, your work is nearly done in advance. I find that combining simple recipes with quality ingredients is a foolproof way of creating a fabulous meal.

After much thought, I have decided to break this chapter down into seasonal categories. I'm a great believer in staying true to the time of year, as each season is bursting with its own flavors. Tomatoes ripened in the summer sun taste divine, just as comforting casseroles with rich flavors embrace the winter. It's my aim to incorporate seasonal flavors and moods into each one of these dinner-party dishes, from the appetizer through to the dessert.

spring menu

roasted asparagus with hollandaise sauce on toast

If you have locally grown organic asparagus and good-quality bread, this is possibly going to be one of the most delicious tastes you have ever experienced.

serves 4

16 asparagus spears
sea salt
olive oil, for tossing and grilling
8 slices of good-quality bread
   (white sourdough works best)

For the Hollandaise sauce
3½ sticks butter
10 egg yolks
juice of 2 lemons
sea salt and freshly ground black pepper

cook's tip

other dinner-party sauces using hollandaise

For a Creamy Spinach Sauce, blanch a fistful of fresh spinach in boiling water, drain, chop, and stir into a Hollandaise sauce.

For a Béarnaise sauce, cook some white wine or vinegar, diced shallots, tarragon, and peppercorns together in a saucepan, reduce, sieve, and then add to a Hollandaise sauce.

Toss the asparargus spears in a bowl with sea salt and some olive oil. If you have a grill pan, then place it over high heat with some olive oil. When the oil is hot, lie the asparagus spears on top and leave to cook for 3 minutes on each side. If you don't have a grill pan, fill a saucepan about one-third full with water and place over high heat. When the water begins to boil, drop in the asparagus and cook for about 4 minutes (the asparagus is cooked when you can pierce it with a sharp knife).

To make the Hollandaise sauce, melt the butter in a saucepan. While the butter is melting, pour the egg yolks and lemon juice into a food processor. On a medium speed, slowly pour in the melted butter through the nozzle until all the butter is well blended with the egg yolks and the sauce has a thick consistency.

Toast 8 slices of bread and assemble them on a large platter. Place asparagus spears on the platter and season with salt and pepper. Pour the Hollandaise sauce into a bowl and add to the platter.

baked sole with salsa verde

This is one of the simplest ways of cooking fish and, if your fish is spankingly fresh, there is no better way to cook a flat fish in my very humble opinion...The salsa verde is fabulous drizzled over baked fish, but equally good served with broiled chicken or as a dip with vegetable cruditées. It's a great stand-by sauce or dip because it will last for up to 2 weeks in the refrigerator.

serves 4

1 whole sole, approx. 4lb 8oz
sea salt

Preheat the oven to 400°F.

Score the flesh of the sole quite deeply on both sides, diagonally at 2in intervals. Season well with salt and place the sole pale-skin-side down in a large roasting pan.

Pour in enough water to immerse half of the fish. Bake in the oven for 30 minutes or until the flesh of the fish is cooked. When cooked, the flesh will be white and come away from the bone with ease.

Once the sole is cooked, take from the oven and carefully remove the skin.

Serve with the Salsa Verde (see page 174).

Place the fish fillets on a serving dish and spoon over the Salsa Verde before serving.

lemon sorbet

These are so simple to make—it's just a matter of squeezing, stirring, and freezing! They look so fabulous in their frozen lemon cups. If you don't have the time to make the sorbet, then just fill the cups with good ice cream and serve.

serves 4

1 ⅓ cups superfine sugar
1 ¾ cups water
juice of 6 lemons (cut the lemons in half through the center)
grated zest of 2 lemons

Pour the sugar and water into a saucepan and place over medium heat. Bring to a boil, stirring every few minutes until all the sugar has dissolved.

Take off the heat and stir in the lemon juice and zest.

Pour into a large plastic container and let cool.

Once cooled, put the sorbet in a freezer, stirring every 30 minutes so that no large ice crystals form.

While the sorbet is setting, scoop out the fibers from the halved lemons and slice off just enough of the bottoms of the lemons so that they will stand upright. Put in the freezer.

Once the sorbet has set, scoop into the frozen lemon cups and serve straight away.

roasted tomato and basil soup

I came up with this recipe when I was living in Italy. The base of the soup also makes the perfect topping for a bruschetta; just follow the recipe up until the point of adding the stock. Then, serve cold over toasted sourdough bread that's been brushed with olive oil.

serves 4

1¼lb cherry tomatoes, halved
2 garlic cloves, crushed
1 red onion, chopped into large chunks
sea salt and freshly ground black pepper
extra virgin olive oil, for drizzling
1 tablespoon balsamic vinegar
10 fresh basil leaves, torn
2 cups chicken or vegetable stock

Preheat the oven to 325°F.

Put the tomatoes, garlic, and onion in an ovenproof dish, season with salt and pepper, and drizzle with olive oil and balsamic vinegar.

Using clean hands, massage all the ingredients together for 5 minutes to enhance the flavor of the soup. Roast in the oven for 20 minutes.

Allow the tomatoes to cool slightly once they have come out of the oven, then place them into a large bowl with the fresh basil leaves. Allow the basil to infuse the tomatoes. I usually do this for about 1 minute.

Pour the chicken stock into a saucepan, stir in the tomatoes and basil, and place over low heat for 20 minutes.

To serve, place a piece of toasted baguette on top with melted Parmesan cheese.

spicy crab linguine

This recipe is so light and refreshing. I love eating it in the summer. It's fantastic if you can get fresh crab, but there are also lots of great companies selling vacuum-packed cooked crab.

serves 4

1¼lb linguine
olive oil, for frying
1 scallion, finely sliced
1 red chile, finely chopped
10½oz cooked crab meat
grated zest and juice of 1 lemon
sea salt and freshly ground
   black pepper
bunch of fresh cilantro,
   roughly chopped

Put the linguine in a large saucepan of salted boiling water. Stir for a minute, let cook for a further 5 minutes, and then drain.

Meanwhile, place a large skillet over medium heat and pour in some olive oil. Stir in the scallions and chile, and let simmer for 3 minutes.

Place the cooked crab into the pan with the chile and scallion.

Pour over the lemon juice, stir, and let cook for 2–3 minutes. Fold in the linguine.

Season with salt and pepper, and transfer to a serving dish.

Sprinkle the lemon zest and fresh cilantro over the dish before serving.

rose-water gelatin

Bring back the jello! It looks and tastes so decadent. They tick all my boxes—easy to make, delicious, cheap, and old-fashioned.

serves 4

For the crystallized rose petals
1 egg white
2 teaspoons water
12 rose petals (3 for each serving)
¼ cup superfine sugar

For the gelatin
generous 1 cup superfine sugar
2 cups boiling water
approx. ½oz gelatin sheets
scant ¼ cup rose water

To make the crystallized rose petals, mix the egg white and water together in a small bowl. Grip the petals with a pair of tweezers and carefully dip the petals into the egg mixture, lightly coating both sides.

Dip the rose petals very lightly in the superfine sugar and transfer to a wire rack. Let the petals dry overnight or for about 6 hours.

To make the gelatin, stir the sugar and boiling water together in a saucepan. Keep stirring until the sugar has dissolved, then remove from the heat.

Put the gelatin sheets into a bowl of cold water for 1 minute or until soft, drain and stir into the syrup until dissolved.

Stir in the rose water and let cool. Pour the cooled syrup into 4 individual glasses and put into the refrigerator to set (this takes about 1 hour).

Arrange 3 crystallized rose petals on each glass of gelatin, and serve.

variation
Put 3 raspberries in each of the 4 glasses and pour the jelly syrup half way up the glass. Put in the refrigerator to set and then put another 3 raspberries on top, followed by more syrup, until the glasses are full. Leave to set as above.

.... cook's tip ....

making some crystallized flowers

All these flowers can be crystallized and then used to decorate cakes and gelatin: nasturtiums, marigolds, pansies, roses, calendulas, cornflowers, and violets. Be sure that they were not sprayed with pesticides, and wash them gently before using.

fall menu

wild mushroom, parmesan, and arugula bruschetta

There are lots of different toppings for a bruschetta, including the traditional tomato and basil or roasted asparagus and feta cheese.

serves 4

olive oil
14oz mixed wild mushrooms (such as porcini, oyster, chanterelle, and morel)
sea salt and freshly ground black pepper
juice of ½ lemon
8 slices of sourdough bread
2oz Parmesan cheese

Place a skillet over medium heat and drizzle in some olive oil. When the oil is hot, add the mushrooms, season with salt and pepper, and squeeze over the lemon juice. Let cook for 3–5 minutes, tossing all the time.

Toast the sourdough bread on both sides and drizzle with a little olive oil.

When the mushrooms are cooked, divide them between the 8 slices of toasted bread.

Place slivers of Parmesan cheese over the mushrooms (I find that my vegetable peeler is the best utensil for this).

italian beef stew

This is a great dish to serve when you are cooking for more than two people. It tastes even better when you cook it the day before. It's delicious served with olive roast potatoes (see my recipe for Lemon and Thyme Roasties on page 87) and just replace the lemon and thyme with scant ⅓ cup of black olives, chopped.

serves 6

2 tablespoons olive oil
1 onion, thinly sliced
2 garlic cloves, crushed
1 red bell pepper, seeded and thinly sliced
3lb 5oz stewing beef, cut into chunks
1 tablespoon all-purpose flour
sea salt and freshly ground black pepper
2¾ cups fresh button mushrooms, sliced
¾ cup + 2 tablespoons red wine
2 x 14oz cans of chopped tomatoes
2 teaspoons finely chopped
    fresh rosemary

Preheat the oven to 350°F.

Place a flameproof Dutch oven over medium heat and add the olive oil, onion, garlic, and red bell pepper. Cover and cook for 2–3 minutes.

Toss the chunks of beef in the flour, making sure they are thoroughly coated.

Remove the lid from the Dutch oven, add the beef, season with salt and pepper, and brown the meat on all sides.

Add the sliced mushrooms and let cook for a further minute.

Pour in the red wine and let simmer for 10 minutes.

Stir in the tomatoes and rosemary.

Cook in the oven for 1½ hours.

This tiramisù recipe is the best you'll taste. I became obsessed with finding a good tiramisù recipe when I lived in Turin. Often, when you eat it outside of Italy, it is soaked in Amaretto or other liqueurs but, on researching it, I found that the most authentic tiramisù is made without alcohol. The real foodies say it's about the combination of good coffee, the subtle flavor of the mascarpone, and the velvet sprinkling of unsweetened cocoa powder on top. It should be really light and the flavors pronounced—Italian food is all about being able to taste each individual flavor, rather than being bombarded by a strong alcoholic taste.

serves 6

tiramisù

3 egg yolks
⅛ cup superfine sugar
2 cups mascarpone
  cheese
¾ cup + 2 tablespoons
  strong coffee
  or espresso, cold
14 ladyfingers
1¾ cups unsweetened
  cocoa powder

Using an electric hand mixer, beat the egg yolks and superfine sugar together in a large bowl until pale and thick.

Add the mascarpone cheese and whisk slowly until the mixture is pale and smooth. Stir in a scant ¼ cup of the coffee.

Dip half of the ladyfingers into the coffee mixture. Place equal amounts into the bottom of 4 glass coffee cups or small bowls. Alternatively, put the ingredients in a single glass bowl to make one large tiramisù.

Spoon over half the mascarpone mix and sprinkle with half the cocoa powder. Repeat with another layer of ladyfingers, mascarpone mix, and cocoa powder.

Cover and refrigerate for 2 hours, then dust with cocoa powder before serving.

french onion soup with emmenthal toasties

The trick with this soup is to caramelize the onions very well because this is where all the flavor is coming from. The onions should be a dark golden color before the stock is added.

serves 4

¾ stick butter
drop of olive oil
7 cups thinly sliced onions
2 garlic cloves, crushed
1 teaspoon sugar
¼ cup + 2 tablespoons white wine
3¼ cups good-quality beef stock
¾ cup grated Emmenthal cheese
4 slices of baguette

Place a heavy-bottomed saucepan over medium heat and add the butter and olive oil. Once melted, stir in the onions and garlic.

Stir in the sugar and let the onions sauté and then caramelize, stirring every few minutes until they become a deep golden color.

Pour in the white wine and let simmer for 5 minutes before pouring in the beef stock. Let cook for 30 minutes.

Sprinkle the Emmenthal cheese on top of the slices of baguette and put under a broiler to melt.

Serve the onion soup in heated bowls and put the toasted Emmenthal bread on top. Yum!

provençal chicken casserole

This is traditionally cooked using red wine, but I love the flavor of the white wine with the thyme and garlic. If you are going to use red wine, then add some black olives to the casserole. Either way, it's absolutely delicious!

serves 4

1 tablespoon olive oil
1 whole organic or free range chicken, jointed into 8 pieces
4 garlic cloves, whole
16 shallots, peeled
sea salt and freshly ground black pepper
1¾ cups dry white wine
1½ cups chicken stock
bunch of fresh tarragon, roughly chopped

Preheat the oven to 300°F.

Place a flameproof Dutch oven over medium heat and add the olive oil. When the oil is hot, add the chicken pieces and brown lightly.

Add the garlic and shallots, season with salt and pepper, and let cook for a further minute.

Pour the wine over the chicken and let simmer for 10 minutes. Pour in the chicken stock.

Add the tarragon, stir, and cover.

Cook in the oven for 1½ hours.

chocolate and cardamom mousse cups

Make these the night before and then that's one less thing to worry about... Use good-quality chocolate and serve the mousses in your prettiest glasses or cups, and you can't go wrong.

serves 4

7oz good-quality dark chocolate (minimum 70% cocoa solids)
½ cup + 2 tablespoons half and half
4 eggs, separated
1 teaspoon superfine sugar
½ teaspoon cardamom seeds

Break the chocolate into a heatproof glass bowl suspended over a saucepan of simmering water. Stir often to make sure that no lumps form.

Remove from the heat and stir in the half and half, egg yolks, sugar, and cardamom seeds.

In a clean bowl, whisk the egg whites until they form stiff peaks.

Fold the whisked eggs into the chocolate mixture.

Pour the chocolate mixture into individual glasses or cups and place in the refrigerator for 1 hour or until set.

cook's tip

serving mousses

Use espresso cups, martini glasses, or china cups for serving your mousses in, to create a decadent look.

If you are serving mousses for a dinner party, then make them the night before so that you aren't stuck in the kitchen for hours!

variation
To make a fruit mousse, leave out the spice and instead fold in fresh raspberries or strawberries.

homemade edible gifts

Finding a perfect gift for a friend or loved one that is both meaningful and well liked is no easy feat. On many occasions, I have tirelessly walked up and down the main street in search of that one perfect gift and, more often than not, I've returned home disappointed or even worse—giftless!

More recently, however, I have traded in the hours and expense of panicked gift shopping in favor of something I love—cooking—and I have to tell you that within your kitchen cabinets are the best gifts one could ever receive. What better gift can there be, for example, than giving homemade truffles to a chocolate-lover in a fabulously decorated box or some freshly made biscottis to complement a coffee-lover's morning coffee? The whole idea of making a gift from scratch is incredibly refreshing. I have always found that food, whether savory or sweet, has a way of connecting people unlike any other gift you can find.

In this chapter I have given you some of my favorite edible gifts and some ideas on how to make them look beautiful. I hope this will not only inspire you, but will also make your life a little bit easier. The possibilities are endless and the results are priceless.

summer basil pesto

This is another great sauce to learn if you are new to cooking. Homemade basil pesto is incredibly versatile and greatly improves the taste and appearance of any number of dishes. It goes very well with fish, pasta, and chicken. I also use it on salads, crostinis, and even in soups. Best of all, it only takes a few minutes to make and will keep in the refrigerator for up to 3 weeks.

makes generous ³/₄ cup

4½ cups fresh basil leaves
⅔ cup extra virgin olive oil
2 garlic cloves
¼ cup pine nuts
½ cup freshly grated Parmesan cheese
1 teaspoon sea salt

Blend the basil leaves, olive oil, garlic, pine nuts, Parmesan cheese, and salt in a food processor.

And, that's it!

variations
Substitute the basil with cilantro or parsley.

Add 2oz of soft goat cheese and replace the basil with cilantro, and you have a deliciously creamy cilantro pesto that is fantastic with chicken or pasta.

-------- cook's tip --------

preparing your jars

Be sure to sterilize all containers thoroughly before filling. Look for unusual bottles and jars and fill them with delicious homemade chutneys, jams, and sauces.

fall compote

There is a feel-good factor about fall pickings: windfall apples, hedgerows laden with plump blackberries, a neighbor's tree weighed down with ripe pears. It isn't just because the produce is free. I think it's more primal than that. Very few of us hunt for our food anymore, or grow our own, but come fall we can go gathering. There is little to compare with the satisfaction of eating a blackberry and apple pie made with fruit you picked yourself. This compote is the essence of fall. It is delicious whirled through Greek yogurt or scooped over a scone with lashings of cream, but also fabulous served with roast pork.

makes 10 x scant 1 cup jars

scant ½ cup (just over ¾ stick) butter
1lb 10oz apples, peeled, cored, and cubed
½ cup superfine sugar
1 vanilla bean, split
1¾ cups blackberries

Melt the butter in a stainless-steel saucepan. Add the apples, sugar, and vanilla bean, and cook for about 20 minutes.

Just before taking the apples off the heat, stir in the blackberries and continue to cook for a further 5 minutes. The texture should be nice and thick; if not, cook for a further few minutes.

After removing the vanilla bean, transfer the mixture to a food processor or blender, and blend for a few minutes.

Press the mixture through a sieve and store in sterilized jars in the refrigerator for up to 2 weeks.

cook's tip

blackberry foraging and freezing

When picking blackberries, choose the ones at the top, as they haven't had much contact with rodents! Rinse them gently in a colander and eat that day or the next. To freeze the blackberries, spread them out on a flat tray, cover with plastic wrap and put in the freezer.

chocolate pistachio truffles

Melt-in-the-mouth chocolate truffles. Now, who wouldn't want to receive these as a gift? There are so many variations, so this is a great recipe for making in large quantities as you can split the mixture and add different flavorings.

makes 14

7oz good-quality dark chocolate (minimum 70% cocoa solids), broken into pieces
½ cup + 2 tablespoons heavy cream
1 ¼ cups pistachio nuts, finely chopped

Slowly melt the chocolate in a heatproof bowl suspended over a saucepan of simmering water until it is smooth and glossy.

Gently heat the cream in a heavy-bottomed saucepan until warm.

Pour the warm cream onto the melted chocolate and mix well until fully incorporated.

Mix in two-thirds of the pistachio nuts. Set aside to cool and firm up (you can refrigerate the mixture to speed up the process if desired).

Once firm, take teaspoons of the mixture and roll into walnut-sized balls, then leave to set on a tray lined with parchment paper.

Once set, place the remaining finely chopped pistachio nuts in a bowl and roll the truffles in the nuts.

variations
There are so many variations for this recipe. Try replacing the pistachios with hazelnuts or almonds. To spice this up, replace the hazelnuts with 4 cardamon pods or 1 teaspoon of ground cinnamon. Also try adding 2 teaspoons of bourbon, Grand Marnier, rum, or the zest and juice of an orange.

vanilla fudge

Homemade fudge is so superior to the store-bought version. You will need a candy thermometer for this recipe, but it's a good tool to have in the kitchen anyway and it isn't expensive.

makes 24

½ cup + 2 tablespoons milk
½ cup + 2 tablespoons heavy cream
1¼ cups superfine sugar
¾ stick butter
1 teaspoon vanilla extract

Place the milk and cream in a heavy-bottomed saucepan, add the sugar and butter, and bring to a boil over medium heat.

When the mixture comes to a boil, reduce the heat and let simmer for 15 minutes. Remove from the heat and let cool.

The mixture needs to reach "soft-ball" stage, which is at 239°F. Once this is reached, stir in the vanilla extract.

Beat the mixture with a whisk until it reaches a thick consistency. Pour the mixture into a greased baking sheet and let set.

Cut into squares. Store in an airtight container for up to 2 weeks.

variations
Stir ½ cup of rum-soaked raisins into the mix for fudge with a richer flavor. For chocolate fudge, simply stir in 3oz of melted good-quality chocolate. For both these variations, stir in the chocolate or raisins after you have simmered the fudge mix.

christmas cookie dough

Cookie dough makes a delicious and thoughtful gift all year round. Patterned wrapping paper, stationery, and cheerful scraps of paper look so lovely wrapped around rolls of cookie dough that have been bundled in parchment paper.

makes 3 rolls of cookie dough

2¼ sticks butter, softened
½ cup superfine sugar
2½ cups all-purpose flour
1 teaspoon baking powder
3oz white chocolate
½ cup dried cranberries, chopped

Put the butter and sugar in a large bowl and cream together with a wooden spoon until pale in color.

Sift the flour and baking powder, then add the white chocolate and dried cranberries. Bring the mixture together to form a dough.

Cut the dough in three. Roll each third into a sausage shape. Wrap in parchment paper, cover with another wrap of Christmas gift-wrapping paper, and tie at both ends with some pretty ribbon.

Write a little note on a card to say that the cookies should be cut into 8 pieces and then cooked for 10–15 minutes in a preheated oven at 350°F. The dough should be stored in the refrigerator and will keep for up to a week.

hot chocolate mix

This takes just minutes to make, so this is the perfect solution if you are under pressure but still want to make a gift. Just buy some pretty bags for the mix and tie each bag with a ribbon.

makes approx. 9oz

1½ cups good-quality cocoa powder
6oz good-quality semi-sweet chocolate, chopped
¼ cup sugar
1½ tablespoons ground cinnamon
1½ tablespoons pure vanilla extract
1 teaspoon ground nutmeg

Place all the ingredients in a food processor and mix until powdery.

The mix will last for up to 6 months in an airtight container.

meringues

Add a teaspoon of rose water, lavender water, or orange blossom to the meringue mix while you are beating it. You can also try folding in 2oz of finely chopped hazelnuts or almonds, chocolate morsels, or pistachios.

makes 32

4 egg whites
¼ cup superfine sugar
1 cup confectioners' sugar

Preheat the oven to 225°F.

Line 2 baking sheets with parchment paper.

Place the egg whites in a large, clean mixing bowl (not plastic). Beat on medium speed with an electric hand whisk until the mixture resembles fluffy clouds and stands up in stiff peaks when the blades are lifted. Turn up the speed and start to add the superfine sugar, a spoonful at a time.

Continue beating for 3–4 seconds between each addition. It's important to add the superfine sugar slowly as it helps to prevent the meringue from "weeping" later. However, don't overbeat. When ready, the mixture should be thick and glossy.

Sift a third of the confectioners' sugar over the mixture, then gently fold it in with a big metal spoon or rubber spatula. Continue to sift and fold in the confectioners' sugar a third at a time. Again, don't overmix. The mixture should now look smooth and billowy.

Scoop up a tablespoonful of the mixture. Using another spoon, ease it onto the baking sheet to make an oval shape. Or, just drop them in rough rounds, if you prefer.

Bake in the oven for 1¼ hours until the meringues sound crisp when tapped underneath and are a pale coffee color.

Let cool on the sheets or a wire rack. (The meringues will now keep in an airtight container for up to 2 weeks or frozen for a month.)

orange and almond biscottis

These will keep for up to 2 weeks in an airtight container, so you can make them ahead of time. They are also delicious halved and then dipped in melted chocolate.

makes 36

2 cups all-purpose flour
½ teaspoon baking powder
½ teaspoon baking soda
1 stick unsalted butter, softened
⅔ cup superfine sugar
2 large eggs
2 tablespoons grated orange zest
1 tablespoon orange juice
1 cup whole almonds

Preheat the oven to 350°F.

Sift the flour, baking powder, baking soda, and salt into a large bowl, and mix well.

In a separate bowl, using an electric hand mixer on medium speed, cream together the butter and sugar until light and fluffy.

Beat in the eggs, one at a time, then add the orange zest and juice. Stir into the flour mixture and almonds until the dough comes together.

With floured hands, divide the dough in half. Shape each half into a log and place the logs on a baking sheet with 3in between them. Pat into 3in wide loaves.

Bake in the oven for 30 minutes or until the dough is firm to the touch. Transfer the loaves to a cutting board. Leave the oven on.

Using a serrated knife, cut each loaf crosswise on the diagonal into ½in slices.

Arrange the slices in one layer on a baking sheet. Return to the oven and bake for 10 minutes. Turn the biscotti over and bake for a further 10 minutes.

Transfer the biscotti to wire racks to cool. Store in layers in an airtight container.

cook's tip

gift-wrapping cookies

Put your homemade cookies in colored paper liners encircled with a matching ribbon. Put the filled liners in a see-through bag. String a card with a note of the recipe and a glittery initial of the recipient on a ribbon, and secure the bag with a bow. Gorgeous!

index

acknowledgments

When you write a book it's like going on a journey and lucky for me on my journey I met the most wonderful and inspiring people that have helped in small and large ways to make *Homemade* the book that I dreamed of creating… My first thank you goes to the most creative, inspiring, energizing lady in publishing, Kyle Cathie—thank you from the deepest part of my heart for taking on my dream of a book and making it a reality; you're an incredible woman. Alberto Peroli, who is and will always remain in my eyes the most fabulously talented photographer that I have ever had the pleasure to work with. How you manage to always capture what I ask is incredible, thank you for being so patient with me… Polly Webb-Wilson, thank you so much for pouring all your creativity and calm energy into those two weeks we spent photographing *Homemade* in France. Mum, what can I say about my Mum, well she came with me to France where we shot the book and she cleaned and cooked and made sure everything ran smoothly, oh and she also became the in-house counsellor for those stressful times! A huge thanks and applause to Mark Latter and Caroline West for their incredible graphic talent in making this book look so beautiful! And to Catharine Robertson at Kyle Cathie, for your patience. To my agent and dear friend Noel Kelly, thank you endlessly for all your support and faith, what did I do without you? And of course Niamh Kirwan at NK Management, you have been a dream to work with… And last but by no means least, my two rocks; Judith Kelly, for being such a wonderful colleague and best friend and Peter Gaynor, for giving me so much love and support.